TJ Higgs discovered her psychic powers as a child but, owing to discouragement and a difficult upbringing, it was not until many years later that she really took flight with her gift. Today, she is one of the most successful mediums in the UK. She has appeared on TV in shows such as *Psychic Private Eyes* and *The Three Mediums*, and her work is featured widely in the media. She is the author of *Living with the Gift* and *Signs from the Afterlife*. She runs her own centre for psychic development in Hertfordshire, UK, and tours the country speaking to packed venues. See www.tjhiggs.co.uk for more information.

TRUE SPIRIT

Secrets of the Afterlife

TJ Higgs

LONDON · SYDNEY · AUCKLAND · JOHANNESBURG

1 3 5 7 9 10 8 6 4 2

Published in 2013 by Rider, an imprint of Ebury Publishing
A Random House Group Company

The Random House Group Limited Reg. No. 954009

Addresses for companies within the Random House Group can be found at
www.randomhouse.co.uk

A CIP catalogue record for this book is available from the British Library

The Random House Group Limited supports The Forest Stewardship
Council® (FSC®), the leading international forest certification organisation.
Our books carrying the FSC label are printed on FSC®-certified paper. FSC is
the only forest-certification scheme supported by the leading environmental
organisations, including Greenpeace. Our paper procurement policy can be found
at www.randomhouse.co.uk/environment

Printed and bound in Great Britain by CPI Group (UK) Ltd, Croydon, CR0 4YY

ISBN 9781846043697

To buy books by your favourite authors and register for offers visit
www.randomhouse.co.uk

*The stories in this book are based upon real events. However, some names and details
have been changed to protect the privacy of those involved.*

This book is dedicated to
everyone who has touched my journey with spirit,
adding not only to my vocabulary
but to my soul...

CONTENTS

ACKNOWLEDGEMENTS

Once again I am blessed to be able to share my gift and stories with you.

Many thanks to the team at Rider and in particular Judith Kendra and Sue Lascelles for their support, professional guidance and for believing in me.

To Mary Pachnos at Aitken Alexander Associates for her support and for guiding me along my literary path!

And especially huge thanks to Garry Jenkins, who went above and beyond the call of duty when working with me on this book. A very special man indeed.

Thank you to everyone who has contributed to the writing of *True Spirit* – both from this side of life and from the Afterlife; for allowing me to share my gift and evidence that life truly is eternal.

Love and thanks to Daisie, who has been with me now for the last three years ... Not only a colleague but very much like a daughter to me.

Love and thanks to my beautiful sons, James and Ryan, for enriching my life in so many ways and for their understanding and support of my work.

INTRODUCTION

I first sensed my ability to connect with the spirit world when I was a little girl, growing up in north London. When I was just four, I saw my 'Pops', my great-grandfather, on the day of his funeral. He was sitting there, larger than life, on a chair in the living room while everyone else milled around him dressed in black. I viewed the world very differently from that day on. That's when I first understood that death doesn't mark the end of our existence. And that's when I realised that there is an Afterlife, inhabited by the spirits of our loved ones. What I didn't fully grasp at that young age was how my life would be inextricably linked to this other world. At that point, I didn't fully understand that I was different, and that I was gifted with the ability to connect and communicate with these spirits.

It was only later in my life, in my twenties, that I began to see how I might be able to use that ability to help others as a psychic medium. Since then I have conveyed thousands of messages from the Other Side, learning something new about the vast world that exists beyond what we call death on an almost daily basis.

One thing you can definitely say about being a medium is that you never, ever know what lies around the corner. My psychic life has been a non-stop journey of discovery, full of unpredictable twists and turns. No two days are alike. Come to think of it, no two hours are alike. As you can imagine, it has been quite a ride.

With each passing year, however, there is one thing that becomes more and more obvious to me. The more people I meet either at my public demonstrations or during my private sittings or workshops and teaching sessions, the more I see that there are so many misconceptions and misleading ideas about the spirit world and mediumship. So few people know the truth about what lies beyond this life.

In many ways this isn't surprising, of course. It's not something that's taught in schools or even features on mainstream television or in the media generally. The world of mediumship, and Spiritualism in particular, is also quite a closed, secretive one, in many ways. It's also full of rules and regulations, far too many of them for my liking. But I am still surprised at some of the strange, misguided – and sometimes ridiculous – ideas that people have about mediums, mediumship and the spirit world in general.

This book is my attempt to correct this. I want it to fill in the gaps in people's understanding. I want to tackle some of the most common misconceptions and mistaken beliefs about the spirit world and how it works. But I also want to answer some of the most common questions that

I am asked on a daily basis, from 'do pets go to spirit when they die?' to 'do spirits communicate with us while we are asleep?' (The answer to both those questions is *yes*, by the way.)

Of course, all mediums have slightly different views of the Afterlife. That's inevitable, given the infinite number of possible experiences we can have when communicating with the spirit world. So this is very much my personal view of how it all works. Having said that, it is a view that is based entirely on my own true-life experiences, on the things I have seen, heard and felt during my many years as a psychic medium. It is my view of what represents true spirit.

PROLOGUE:
The Beetle and the Dragonfly

'We need to remember that we are spiritual beings spending some time in a human body.' Barbara de Angelis

I'd like to begin with a story. It's a parable really, one that I heard many years ago and that has come to mean a great deal to me.

Once upon a time, there lived a little water beetle. Its home was in the muddy waters underneath the lily pads in a small pond, where it lived with a community of water beetles. The little beetle and its family and friends lived very comfortably and quietly there; no one disturbed them and they didn't disturb anybody else in return. There was only one dark cloud that hung over the community.

Every now and again, one of the beetles would climb the stem of one of the lily pads and disappear above the surface of the water to sit on the flat leaf of the pad above. They would never be seen again.

This made the water beetles very sad whenever it happened because they believed that it meant their friend was dead and gone for ever.

One day, the little water beetle found himself drawn to the stem of one of the lilies. He felt the irresistible urge to climb up it, and began scaling his way up the long, green shoot. As he climbed, he made a promise to himself: if he got to the top he would make sure not to leave for ever. He would come back and tell his friends what he had discovered at the top of the lily, above the water's surface. This proved easier said than done, however.

When he reached the top and climbed out onto the surface of the lily pad, the little water beetle was so tired and the sun was so hot that he decided to take a little nap. As he lay there, snoozing away in the radiant sunshine, his body changed. When he woke up, he had been transformed into a beautiful blue-tailed dragonfly with broad wings. His body was completely different. Before, he was an oval-shaped beetle with short, stubby legs. Now he was a slender dragonfly, designed to take to the air. And that's exactly what he did. He flew into the air, soaring high into the sky.

As he climbed he turned and looked down on a whole new world. He realised immediately that this was a far superior way of life to the one he and his friends and family had lived underwater. They simply didn't know this life existed.

It was at that moment that it dawned on him what all his friends and family would now be thinking. 'Oh no, they are now really upset because they believe I am dead,' he thought to himself. 'I must go back and tell them I am all right.'

But he couldn't go back. Try as he might, he couldn't get his new body and new wings to penetrate the surface of the water. So he couldn't get back down to his friends and family to explain that, rather than being dead, he was more alive than ever. He couldn't explain that his life was being fulfilled in a new and exciting way.

For a moment, he felt sad, but then he realised something else: there was no need for sadness at all. He now understood that his friends' and family's time would come too. One day, when they were ready, they too would climb up the stalk of the water lily and experience what he'd experienced. They too would raise their wings and begin this joyous and wonderful new life.

There was no need to feel sorrow, only joy.

That story has remained one of my favourites for many reasons. Dragonflies have long played an important part in my life. I became fascinated by their power when I began studying Native Americans and their belief in the spirit qualities of animals. According to Native American tradition, the dragonfly is connected with illusion and separates the truth from what is false. Their most fundamental spiritual meaning is to show the truth.

Being truthful about the spirit world and its meaning is central to what I do. For this reason, the centre at which I practise is called the Dragonfly Centre. But I also love the story of the beetle and the dragonfly because it perfectly sums up the first – and perhaps most important – piece of knowledge about the spirit world, knowledge that eludes so many people.

When we come to the end of our lives on this earth, we pass over into another realm, the spirit world. This is a wonderful, beautiful event. The only sadness about it is that we cannot turn back and let our loved ones know that we are moving on. They are left behind to mourn us and to miss us. But if they knew that this is where we were, and that, one day, they will all join us on our miraculous journey, they would feel very differently about this life – and the next.

PART ONE:
The Truth about the Spirit World

'Seeing death as the end of life is like
seeing the horizon as the end of the ocean.'
David Searls

Spirit Truth: the spirit world is similar to this one

When people ask me what the spirit world is like, I think most of them expect me to come out with some dramatic description straight out of a Hollywood movie. They are waiting for me to describe another dimension filled with light and clouds and ethereal music. So I'm sure a lot of them are slightly confused – and probably a bit disappointed – when I tell them that, actually, I see the spirit world as being a lot like this world. And I see it that way because I believe it is a part of this world, not a totally separate one.

I have felt this way ever since I had my first psychic experience, when I was a young child. It was on the day that my great-grandfather, my Pops as I called him, passed over. I saw him sitting in my grandparents' house on the day of his funeral as if it was a normal Sunday afternoon. There was nothing different at all about him. All that was new was that I could see him and no one else could. Ever since then, the spirit world has presented itself to me in this way. Often I see spirits physically present, moving around this world as if they were part of it.

It's not always the case, of course. I am not like the kid from the movie *The Sixth Sense*. I don't 'see dead people' twenty-four hours a day. As a psychic and a medium I tune into other things. So at other times I hear the voices of spirits or sense their feelings. Sometimes I hear music, smell, hear or see things that suggest their presence, and the message they want to convey. Whatever the means of communication, however, I always have the sense that they are close at hand, around us in the same way that the weather is always around us. As I say, they are part of this world, living a parallel existence to us – not cast away in some other, distant dimension.

Of course, not everyone agrees with this view. A lot of mediums have different ideas about what lies on the Other Side of this life. Some believe that we are reincarnated, for instance. The *whole* of our being returns to this world, only in a new form. Now I have to lay my cards on the table here: I simply can't understand this idea. My main problem is this: if the whole of us is reincarnated, how is it that, when I am working as a medium, I'm communicating with someone in the other world? How can that be happening if the person has reincarnated back to this world? Who is communicating? Who are we talking to? I'll explain a little more about my thoughts on what actually happens here in Part One.

In stark contrast to this view, other mediums argue that we aren't reincarnated at all – that spirits occupy another plane, another dimension that operates at a different frequency. They say that we mediums have the ability to tune into that frequency like a radio. Again, this is something that leaves me scratching my head. I don't understand that at all because of my personal experience of communicating with the spirit world. I know that if I want to talk to someone's relative I just ask them to come and stand beside me. I don't need to communicate with another plane. (I don't actually use that word 'plane', in fact. When my students use it I tell them we're on the earth – not a plane, not a jumbo jet.)

TRUFFLE'S SPOT

You don't need to be a psychic medium to understand that there are times when we all instinctively know that something is wrong. I'm sure we've all had that feeling in our bones, when, even though we can't see or hear anything, we just feel something awful has happened.

One such moment came on a November morning when I sensed something was terribly amiss the moment

I woke up. I'd allowed myself a bit of a lie-in following a late finish working at a demonstration far from home the previous night. When I heard the knock, however, I knew I had to get up immediately. I arrived downstairs to find both my sons, James and Ryan, crying their eyes out.

'What's happened?' I said.

'I'm afraid there's been an accident. It's Truffle,' the neighbour said.

I felt sick to my stomach immediately. Truffle was my favourite cat. I have had a number of lovely cats over the years, but she was the one with the biggest personality and the warmest heart.

I only had on my pyjamas and dressing gown but I didn't care. We ran across the road to where I could see Truffle lying inanimate. She didn't look damaged. She still looked perfect. But it was clear that she was dead. The neighbour told me that he'd seen her hit by a speeding white van. Typically, it hadn't slowed down or stopped after the collision, but blithely driven on.

I have to admit I cried openly. With my neighbour's help, I brought Truffle back into the house and wrapped her up, ready to be buried. Still in a bit of state, I went upstairs to have a shower and get properly dressed. When I came out of the shower I saw something I will never forget.

As I went to fetch something from a cupboard, I looked down from the mezzanine part of my living room, to where there is a large sofa. There my other three cats, Belle, Merlin and Tiggs, were all lying in their usual positions. They had left a gap, and in that gap there was a green glow.

It wasn't just me who could see it. I heard Daisie, my son Ryan's girlfriend, saying, 'Look at that!'

It was a profound moment in several ways. First and foremost, of course, it was really comforting at that particular time. It eased the pain of losing Truffle. In fact, it meant that I'd not lost her at all in the spirit sense. That was her spot and the other cats knew it, so she could go there every day if she wanted.

But it also made me think about how her new existence must have looked to her. And from her perspective, it wasn't that different at all. I will look at this subject in more detail later, but it's my firm belief that our pet animals inhabit the same spirit world as us because we have interacted on an emotional level in this life. So what applied to Truffle also applies to each human who crosses over to the Other Side.

We each of us have our place and we are as free to occupy it as spirits as we were before we crossed over. Now, some people may exercise this freedom and stay in this place. But others may not and may choose to exercise the equal freedom they have to inhabit another place.

That evening it struck me that this was a perfect illustration of the way the spirit world works.

Spirit Truth: **this life is where our soul learns**

How do I know that I'm right? What makes me so sure that my interpretation of the Afterlife is correct? Well, those are fair questions, ones that I am asked on a regular basis.

My answer is always the same. My view of the Afterlife is based on first-hand experience and the knowledge that has been passed on to me by the various spirits and spirit guides I have communicated with since I began my development in my early twenties. A couple of my guides are particularly helpful: one of them, an Irishman called, funnily enough, Paddy, and a younger man, Luke, are particularly instructive. It was these two who passed on to me perhaps the most important piece of information that I have learned. And that is the knowledge that a part of the soul comes back and it comes back for a very specific purpose – to learn.

This is where, I think, some other mediums' views of the Afterlife are valid. (Don't get me wrong. I respect and admire the views of many of my colleagues, some of whom have acquired wisdom way beyond that which I've collected in my short time in this world.) Those mediums who believe spirits live elsewhere – on that other, erm, plane – are partly right, I think. The essence of a person exists there. However, I passionately believe that the part of the soul that needs to learn returns to this world. In many ways, this fits in with the religious idea of heaven and hell. If you want to think of it in those terms, this world is the hell part where the soul learns and the spirit world is the heaven where our soul heals.

I realise this might be hard to understand, so let's take an example. Let's consider someone who killed someone else during this life.

I believe that the first thing that happens when you pass over is that you see every bit of pain and every bit of joy and love that you've given in your life. It's almost like you watch a DVD of your life. Your soul gets to feel that. If your soul is full of love and generosity, then it's a pleasant experience. You don't have to be a perfect person to experience this, by the way. We've all upset people and we've all done things we are not proud of, haven't we? But in the main, if we are good people, this will be a positive experience. For others, however, it will not be so pleasant. They will have to make recompense for the bad things they have done. They will then have to come back to this life to feel what they have inflicted. Their soul will feel that. And it will learn from that feeling.

So if you are someone who has inflicted pain in this life, you are going to have to go through and feel the repercussions. You are then going to have to make a bargain or a deal to come back and experience them yourself.

Now, I don't mean that a murderer will come back and be murdered or that a person who is murdered is somebody who committed murder in a previous life. It's much subtler than that. Instead, these souls will come back and, in one form or another, bear witness to suffering in some form. As I say, this life will be the hell that prepares their soul for the heaven where it will be healed – the spirit world.

Spirit Truth: spirits can communicate as soon as they cross over to the Other Side

---

FRESH EARTH

A lot of people labour under all sorts of misapprehensions about the Afterlife. It's not surprising, of course. Why should ordinary people understand the complexities of the other world? How would they know how things work in the life that follows death? What constantly surprises me, however, is how little supposedly knowledgeable people know about the Afterlife.

For instance, I often hear mediums talking about the period of time it takes before a person is ready to communicate from the Other Side. I've heard people talk about lengthy 'transitional periods' that spirits have to go through. Some go so far as to be specific and say it takes six months. As far as I am concerned, this, again, is nonsense. There are no hard and fast rules. A spirit is ready to begin communicating the moment it leaves the body of the person it inhabited during its time on this earth. And time is meaningless on the Other Side.

Fittingly, I learned this at the famous Arthur Findlay

College, near Stansted in Essex, the best-known training centre for mediums and psychics in the country, and maybe even the world.

I trained there when I was a developing medium and took part in a number of really interesting workshops and courses.

It was there that I had a really memorable experience. It happened on a Friday, during one of the demonstrations that the college regularly held at the end of the week. As an 'apprentice' medium I was regularly assessed and this session was part of that ongoing process, so I was a little bit nervous about it.

The first thing that I sensed was a really strong smell, of fresh earth and also really fresh flowers. It was so strong it was as if I'd stepped into the middle of New Covent Garden flower market. I was also aware of a digital clock – it read 1:01.

Now, making sense of this wasn't so easy. But I began to feel a connection with two people, sitting at different ends of the room. That didn't really make much sense to me at first, but when I began to talk to these two I discovered that they were, in fact, brother and sister. They'd sat away from each other partly for that very reason. They didn't want it to be too easy for a medium to put them together.

I asked them whether the things I was seeing made any sense to them. They both nodded.

They told me that their mother had passed at the age of 101 years. They also told me that she had passed in the last week and that the funeral hadn't yet taken place.

That was why I was getting such a strong sense of fresh earth and flowers. It was the funeral. The spirit of their mother also kept showing me the grounds of Stansted Hall, outside the building, so I mentioned this to them. They nodded at this and revealed that she had, like them, had a great belief in the work of mediums and the Spiritualist church and had asked to be buried in the gardens of Stansted Hall.

They told me that they had been trying to get that sorted during this week. It was an important sitting for me in many ways. It impressed the assessors at the college, but more importantly it gave the brother and sister validation that their mother had safely crossed over. They were both extremely grateful for that.

The most lasting lesson, however, was that spirits can communicate very soon. This lady was still lying in the mortuary at a nearby undertakers, but she had already begun communicating with a medium. It changed my outlook about how the spirit world works for ever.

Spirit Truth: you don't need to be religious to believe in the Afterlife

---

'I love you when you bow in your mosque,
kneel in your temple, pray in your church.
For you and I are sons of one religion, and
it is the spirit.' *Khalil Gibran*

One of the things that surprises people about me is that I am not what you would call a religious person. I don't subscribe to a particular faith and wouldn't call myself a Christian or a Muslim, or anything to be honest. Now, the first thing I need to say is that this is not because I don't agree with religion. That's not the case at all. I respect all religions, from Spiritualism and Christianity to Hinduism, Buddhism and Islam.

I also respect and understand why people have their faith and their religion. The teachings of the Bible, the Koran and other holy books give a lot of people a great deal of comfort, strength and a real sense of community. It is a central part of a lot of people's identity. These books are also full of wonderful, beautiful stories and universal messages that we can all draw upon.

But the truth is that I just don't feel I need the support that a lot of people get from religion. Mainly I don't need it because I have faith that there's another world and that we all go there when we leave this one. That faith is underlined by what I do, communicating with spirits in that other world.

But I also don't need it for other reasons.

For a start, religion is full of rules. That's not something I'm comfortable with. As far as I am concerned, there are very few rules in the Afterlife. So I don't see a purpose in my following a set of rules in this life when I don't need them for the next one.

What's more, religion doesn't work for me from a practical point of view. I have clients from all over the world who believe in all sorts of things. I don't want to be governed by a religion and a particular set of restrictions when I speak to these people. The fact that they are Hindu or Jewish, Christian or Muslim, is of no consequence to me when they are sitting in front of me. Equally my faith is not of any consequence to them.

Now, this can be a problem for some people. Some would prefer it if people like me were governed by some kind of body, in the same way that doctors or psychiatrists are. Many people would prefer it if I were a Spiritualist, for instance.

The Spiritualist church has been the dominant force in mediumship for more than a century in this country and is where the so-called seven principles of Spiritualism were laid down. I don't know who wrote them and I don't know what they are. I just know they are not for me. So when I teach people in a formal way I tell them straightaway that I am not a Spiritualist. I explain that I am not anything. I am me, take it or leave it.

The roots of this philosophy lie back in my early days as a medium. Back then I knew I had a gift for communicating with the spirit world, but had no idea how to harness it and use it for the benefit of others. I was very much an apprentice. I was very raw.

Fortunately my first circle leader, a guy called Barry, taught me some of the most important lessons I would ever learn. He didn't believe in rules. His motto was 'be yourself'. And that's what I've always done.

Now this isn't to say that I haven't studied religions. Quite the opposite. I've studied many religious texts and got a lot out of them. What is interesting to me is that they all have things in common. For instance, they all talk about angels. That suggests to me that it is possible to take a different approach, whilst believing essentially the same thing. My approach is just another variation on some very familiar themes.

As I say, there are a lot of things I like about religion. I love the fact that meditation and peace are at the core of the purest religions, and I love visiting holy places.

One of my favourites in the UK, for instance, is the Neasden Hindu Temple. Whenever I go there I am invited in to sit for prayers, sometimes on my own. Obviously they sense something about me. I'm not ignored because I'm not a Hindu, quite the opposite in fact. I'm encouraged because I'm a spiritual person. Surely that's the way it should be. We should respect what people believe – and also what they need. I love the feeling of love and peace that you get in the Neasden Temple. I feel a real connection with this world – and the next one. Again this proves to me that the spirit world is a universal thing. I don't have to be a Hindu or a Christian or a Muslim to get that.

Spirit Truth: we are all made of energy that cannot be destroyed

---

Of course, many religions are suspicious of people like me, who are able to connect with a world beyond their control and understanding. It's always been that way. There's a quote in Leviticus that says 'the medium or the sorcerer should be stoned to death'. I have to say that this baffles me. I don't understand why what I do is against anyone's religion. All mediums are trying to do is show people that this is not the end, which is the principle that religions are built upon. Christianity is built on the resurrection of Christ, and the disciples seeing his spirit body. What's the difference between their vision of Christ and the spirits that I see on a regular basis?

Perhaps part of the suspicion of mediumship lies in its links all the way back to Celtic pagan beliefs, when people understood the relationship between the living and the dead. Their big festival, Samhain, or the night of the dead, celebrated the ability of spirits to cross from one side of life to the other for one day of the year. Yet despite this suspicion, people of all religions have visited me over the years. They have to be careful, in many cases. Muslims, for instance, are very secretive about it. They don't like people to know. Catholics come even though it's against their religion.

Of course whenever I get into this kind of discussion with someone, the inevitable questions come up: so what do I believe in? Do I believe in God? Well, the truth is that I don't necessarily believe in God as a male deity. But I do believe in an energy that connects all of us. And if you want to call that God then that's fair enough. I call it 'the Source'. This is something that a lot of people do agree with me about – from Spiritualists to scientists.

I studied physics at school and I know that we are all made of energy and cannot be destroyed. When I receive a message from the Other Side, that is what I'm communicating with – that energy.

There was a time when the fact that I was not like everybody else used to worry me. I felt like an outsider. But now I'm rather proud of it. I am no outsider as far as the spirit world is concerned. Spirits are still talking to me and as long as they keep talking to me I will keep working because that's what I'm here for.

PART TWO:
The Truth about Spirits

'Humans are amphibians – half spirit and half animal. As spirits they belong to the eternal world, but as animals they inhabit time.' *C.S. Lewis*

Spirit Truth: **spirits have a purpose**

CONNOR AND DARREN

'What do spirits do during their existence?' It's a question I'm asked every now and again, and one that always surprises me because, once more, it reveals how many people have a fundamental misconception about how the spirit world works. They assume that spirits simply drift aimlessly around the Afterlife. They imagine that they simply exist on the Other Side.

It is a completely misguided idea.

As I've said, it's my belief that the spirit world is very much like this one. And that means that spirits have a purpose, just like we do.

I've had many experiences that have underlined and supported this belief. One of the most striking in recent years came at a demonstration I did in Sussex. It was a Saturday night and the atmosphere within the hall was quite lively. I suddenly felt myself in the presence of a young man called Connor. I'd actually connected with him before, at another demonstration nearby. One of the first things that I had picked up from him during that first connection was the fact that he had passed very quickly. He had shown me an image of him flying, suggesting he'd literally flown over from one side to the other. It turned out he'd died in a tragic accident. He'd been killed instantly.

On that first occasion Connor had connected with his mother. She was there again tonight. The first contact between the two of them had been highly emotional. His mother had been understandably devastated at losing Connor and had lost the will to carry on with her life. Hearing from him and knowing that his existence was continuing somewhere else had lifted an enormous weight off her shoulders. I could see the difference in her tonight.

Connor once more passed on a message of love to his mother. He said how proud he was of the progress she'd made in picking up the pieces of her life since they'd last connected. But he didn't dwell for long. It turned out that he had someone else with him, someone who, he was telling me, had a much greater need to connect than he did on this occasion.

I was being shown the name Darren and I had the unmistakable feeling that he had passed very recently. As sometimes happens, I could smell the aromas of a funeral parlour, which led me to believe he hadn't even been laid to rest. As his energy began to grow, replacing that of Connor, I saw that he had taken his own life. He felt that the world would be better off without him, he told me.

As I began describing him, I looked around the theatre and saw something I don't often see. A group of three young women, sitting towards the rear of the auditorium, were glowing green. They looked like little green aliens – it was very odd. It was absolutely clear to me that they were connected to Darren.

I learned that they were three friends of Darren and were clearly delighted to hear from him. All three of them were crying.

Because he was such a recent arrival in spirit, Darren had little to say beyond the fact that he knew his family were planning his funeral and that they needed to stick together during the next few days. After that, the best thing they could do to honour his memory was to get on with their lives and do the best they could.

As Darren faded, I felt Connor was still with him and was leading him back into the light. He was obviously some kind of guardian or protector and was going to be with Darren during his transition into the spirit world.

The message was a huge comfort for Darren's friends, but, in a curious way, it was an even more reassuring and rewarding message for Connor's mother. The first time she'd heard from him her emotions had been very exposed, she was still in mourning. Now, a few months on, she was delighted to discover that her son had a purpose and that he was helping someone else.

This is a truth that everyone should embrace. When our loved ones cross over to the Other Side, they don't lose their purpose. It's actually quite the opposite: their existence often takes on a real meaning.

Another way of putting it is this: we all have a purpose for being here, but we also have a purpose for not being here any more.

Spirit Truth: **spirits don't lose their personality**

It's common for people to think of spirits as having no character or personality. They think of those who have passed over as bland, ethereal, almost angelic figures. I think this is partly the fault of religion. Angels in religious tradition, for instance, are very anodyne, saintly figures. They are spirits, but they don't seem to have any personality. From my experience of the spirit world, I can tell you that this is very far from the truth. Very far indeed, at times.

As I've explained, the Other Side is a reflection of this world, so it follows that people don't come back from the Afterlife perfect. We are not perfect here in this life, so why should we be in the next life? Besides, if people came back as perfect beings, no one would recognise them.

My granddad was a cantankerous, awkward old so-and-so at times, so if he came back as a really happy, jolly person I'd say, 'Well that's not my granddad.' I loved him as he was. He was hard work in this life – and I'm absolutely certain that he is hard work in the next world as well. And I wouldn't want him any other way.

Day in day out I encounter strong and distinctive characters and personalities. They too can be awkward, pushy or even funny. Some, however, have been more memorable than others.

RING OF FIRE

Anyone who imagined that spirits don't have a sense of humour should have been in the theatre in Birmingham where I received a particularly memorable message one evening.

It all started normally enough. I felt the presence of an elderly man who was giving me the name Jack, along with other names. I sensed that he was an uncle rather than a father. He was suggesting a chain of names that led to someone in the audience. As I began sharing some more information, I felt myself being directed towards a couple sitting just a couple of rows from the front.

It didn't take me more than a split second to work out that the gentleman was a sceptic. The moment I came to them he sat back in his chair and raised his eyebrows at me as if to say, 'Oh, here we go.'

The lady was a little more receptive, however, and accepted some of the evidence I was offering. She confirmed she had had an Uncle Jack. It was at that point that Jack was joined by another man, a very lively character indeed. I pretty quickly identified him as the lady's father-in-law, the sceptical man's father.

I often hear music when I am in the process of trying to interpret a message. Tonight I heard Johnny Cash singing one of his most familiar songs, 'Ring of Fire'. I had absolutely no idea what it meant. I was even more confused when I saw a blow-up ring, the sort you'd give a child in a swimming pool or throw as a lifeline to a drowning person. Again, this didn't make much sense but I thought I'd put it out there and see whether it got a reaction.

It certainly got that.

The minute I described what I was seeing and hearing the man's wife burst out laughing. The father-in-law was laughing almost as hard. Whatever it was he was showing me was absolutely hilarious as far as he was concerned. The one person who wasn't finding this in the slightest bit amusing was the lady's husband. He looked even more uncomfortable than before. He was literally squirming in his seat.

His obvious discomfort was made even worse by the fact that the audience was by now finding all this very entertaining and was giggling. As the wife explained what it was that I was seeing, their giggles were about to turn to howls of laughter.

She told me that they had just been on a very nice cruise – around the Mediterranean, I think it was. But the holiday had been ruined by the fact that her husband had brought the wrong medication for the condition he was suffering from: piles.

At this point, the audience erupted. The man slid into his chair and shot me a look as if he wanted the earth to swallow him up. I couldn't blame him. The father was eager to tell me more, but his son had heard enough.

'Tell my dad that's enough. He's had his laugh, he always loved a joke. Just tell him that's enough,' he said.

A part of me felt a little bit sorry for him, although I soon saw him smiling at his wife as if he'd got the joke. But my main feeling was one of happiness for him. And for his dad.

I got the clear feeling that the dad had held the same opinion of mediums as his son while he'd been here with us. They'd both had those opinions well and truly transformed after their encounter that evening, however. I'm sure the son has never listened to Johnny Cash in the same way again.

CHAIN OF OFFICE

Maybe it's because I lace my demonstrations with a little light comedy, but I do tend to attract some rather mischievous spirits. One of the funniest spirit personalities I have come across presented herself at a church hall in Walsall, where I gave a demonstration a few years ago.

It was quite a high-profile event and there were several members of the local council in the audience, including the Mayor and Mayoress, who were sitting near the front. I didn't need to be psychic to know it was them because they were wearing their bling – both of them had dazzling chains of office around their necks.

There were a couple of ladies sitting with them, as part of the Mayoral party. One was an older lady who had a very regal look. She reminded me a lot of the Queen Mother during her final decades. She was very prim and dignified and was immaculately turned out.

Shortly after I began the demonstration, an elderly woman appeared at the back of the church hall. She too looked very grand. She was dressed in a classic Queen Mum colour – a skirt and jacket of powder blue.

I could tell immediately that she was a very lively soul. The fact that she'd appeared out in the auditorium rather than, as I preferred, behind or alongside me on the stage, told me a lot about her independent spirit. It was soon on display. She began floating from the back towards the front, where the Mayor and his party were sitting. She landed almost on top of the elderly 'Queen Mum' lady, to whom she bore a remarkable resemblance.

It was pretty obvious to me who this lady was.

'Your mother is here,' I said to the lady in the Mayor's party. 'She looks just like you.' It was true. Both the ladies looked very regal.

Her mother was what I like to call a 'queue jumper'. She had no intention of waiting in line with the other spirits who were trying to get through to me on stage. 'Your mother didn't like to queue, did she?' I said.

'No, she didn't,' her daughter laughed.

Her mother was already being very busy in the front rows of the theatre. She began by acknowledging the man sitting next to her daughter, who I sensed was the husband – the spirit's son-in-law. I knew already that he was a senior councillor because he'd been in trouble with the audience earlier in the evening.

Another spirit had come through and had a go at him for not giving his daughter permission to build a path! This had produced some gentle boos from the audience and the guy had been left squirming in his seat. I felt quite sorry for him, truth be told. He'd already been told off publicly and now he had his mother-in-law looking at him as if he had done wrong.

What was really funny about the behaviour of this spirit lady, however, was the way she reacted to the Mayoress, who was sitting a few seats along from her daughter. She was looking at her in a disapproving manner, gently shaking her head at her. It was soon clear what she disliked about the lady. She began leaning over, trying to take the chain of office off the Mayoress. It was obvious to me that she wanted to put it around her daughter's neck.

'Why is your mother trying to pinch the Mayoress's chain so that she can put it around your neck?' I asked the lady.

The Mayor and his party all burst into fits of laughter at this. They were clearly in on a joke that I wasn't privy to. It was only after the demonstration had finished that they let me in on it.

'We were the Mayor and Mayoress until a year or so ago,' the councillor husband of the Queen Mum lady told me. 'Her mum was still alive when we were in office and really loved the fact that her daughter could walk around with a big chain round her neck,' he said. 'She was quite a lady, I can tell you.'

'You don't need to,' I smiled.

THE HELICOPTER RIDE

Messages come to me in all sorts of ways. As well as seeing, hearing and smelling communications from the spirit world, I can also be influenced by thoughts. I can suddenly discover an idea in my head.

Occasionally, I can also be influenced physically. I can start to behave in a way that is somehow related to the message that the spirit wants to get through. And that's precisely what happened one night on a stage in the West Midlands when I suddenly found myself swaying from side to side for no apparent reason. One moment I was standing normally, the next I was rocking around as if I was on a bucking bronco or some mad fairground ride. I'm sure some of the audience must have wondered whether I'd been drinking something stronger than tea during the interval.

I knew it was a communication of some kind but I couldn't make head nor tail of it at that point. I was soon being shown a series of images, but they didn't help much either. All I could see was the 1980s television presenter Anneka Rice and her show *Challenge Anneka*. She was running away from me in a blue jumpsuit.

When I explained all this to the audience they burst into roars of laughter. They must have thought I was losing my mind. It was the next piece of evidence that helped me solve the puzzle of what the communication meant. The story it revealed was far from funny.

I was still rocking from side to side when I began to hear the deafening sound of a helicopter. This obviously was what the spirit had meant when it had shown me *Challenge Anneka*. She famously would jump out of a helicopter each week. As well as this sound, I began to see references to the military. When I described this to the audience, I saw a young man halfway towards the back of the theatre gesturing to me.

'Do you understand this?' I said. 'Because I'm not sure I do.'

'Yes, I do,' he said. 'I think you may have my brother with you.'

The young man was quite composed and matter-of-fact about this. As I connected more deeply with his brother, I saw the pair of them as boys, one laughing and the other looking more serious.

'Your brother was the joker in the family,' I said.

He nodded. 'Yes, it would be typical of him to still be trying to make people laugh now.'

During the next few minutes, I pieced together what had happened. His brother had been serving in Afghanistan when the helicopter he was travelling in ran into severe weather. The pilot had eventually lost control of the chopper and it had crashed into a remote, desert area, killing everyone on board. The rocking sensation that I'd experienced was clearly his way of trying to explain the experience that he'd been through during the final moments of his life.

He wanted to thank his brother for the support he'd been giving his widow and his young son. He also wanted to tell his brother that he was at peace on the Other Side and that his brother didn't need to feel any kind of guilt about what had happened to him.

The brother, as it turned out, was in the military as well and had served two tours of Afghanistan himself. At that point he got quite emotional and began dabbing away tears.

It wasn't the most earth-shattering message. It was one of those communications that conveyed that simplest piece of news: 'I'm here on the Other Side and I'm OK. Don't worry.' What stuck in my mind about it for days afterwards, however, was the fact that it had been delivered with the same humour that had been the brother's trademark during his time here with us. If he'd conveyed his message simply by making me rock from side to side, as he himself had done during his helicopter's descent to disaster, then it would have been a very sombre message. Instead he'd made his communication more light-hearted and positive by including clips from a silly television programme. He almost certainly knew my reputation for drawing on the humour of messages and had banked, quite correctly, on me getting a laugh from Anneka Rice and her jumpsuits.

It illustrated, once more, the fact that spirits don't change their personality when they pass over to the Other Side. Jokers remain jokers, they don't lose their sense of humour – as this very brave and loving young man had proved.

THE MAN FROM LA SENZA

There's something very genuine about spirits who speak exactly as they did during this life – even if they do cause embarrassment to those they have left behind. The spirit of a young man who made himself known to me during a demonstration in Hayes in Middlesex was a perfect illustration of this.

As I sensed his energy initially, I could see a birthday balloon floating above a rather attractive young lady sitting near the front of the theatre. I sensed that he had passed in a tragic accident and that they'd been very much in love when he'd left her, probably a couple of years earlier.

'I need to acknowledge it's your birthday because I have your ex-boyfriend here and he'd like to wish you a happy birthday,' I said to her.

I could see that it was a little bit awkward because she was sitting there with her new bloke. So it was even more awkward when he put the next thought into my head. I had no choice but to say it, of course: 'I loved you, you should have been mine.'

Again, I could see that she was torn by this. Part of her was touched to be getting this communication from someone to whom she had obviously been extremely close. But another part of her was horrified that her current boyfriend was having to hear it.

Things only went from bad to worse, however. It's not often that spirits talk to me about their sex lives. I should explain something here before going on. People always worry that spirits are watching their private moments – whether it is in the bathroom or the bedroom. That's highly unlikely. You have to put it into context. If your parents are in spirit, they aren't going to walk in and watch you when you are on the toilet. Why would they do that in this life? So why would they do that from spirit?

In this case, however, there was no question that the ex-boyfriend had been in her bedroom. I was shocked when I saw the next image he was showing me. I saw the sign for La Senza, the underwear store. He then explained to me, in great detail, that his ex-girlfriend looked very sexy in the new underwear that her boyfriend had bought her. Now I have to say that he didn't do this in any lecherous or unpleasant way. He clearly had been madly in love with this girl and it was obvious that he had loved buying her nice underwear.

Of course, the audience were in hysterics at this. But the poor boyfriend had turned a shade of beetroot. He looked like he wanted the earth to swallow him whole. Fortunately I could tell that they had a solid relationship, one that was going to survive this message. Again, that was part of the beauty of it.

This young man's message was a genuinely loving message, delivered in a way that was true to the spirit of the relationship he'd had with this young girl. And for that reason, it was a message that I was proud to have delivered – despite the embarrassment I caused.

DISORDERLY SPIRITS

As anyone who has seen me demonstrate live will know, I am an unconventional medium in many ways. By this I mean that I am less rigid and disciplined than many of the more polished practitioners of the art. Anything can happen in my demonstrations! I also like to raise a few laughs, which is why some people call me a 'comedium'.

There's a good reason for this, of course. There is a little method in my madness. I've learned over the years that the lighter and happier the atmosphere, the more spirit is drawn to it. More importantly, a joyful and positive vibe within the church or theatre also helps those members of the audience who are tense or apprehensive to relax. That's vital if they are to get the most from any communication that comes their way.

Sometimes, however, I pay the price for my relaxed and less structured methods. I am often prey to what I like to call 'queue jumpers', like the lady in Walsall I mentioned.

I tend to get a lot of these because, unlike other mediums who tend to have gatekeepers who keep some kind of order and ensure that spirits come through in a steady stream, I simply ask spirits to stand behind me. Sometimes they do, but sometimes they don't. Instead they often appear and start floating around the auditorium, or sit on the lap of the person to whom they want to connect. They will do anything to jump the queue, basically. Hence the name 'queue jumpers'.

Of course, it's evidence once again that the spirit world is no different to the world that we inhabit. Here we have people who will stand patiently in a queue and won't push themselves forward. But we also have people who are attention seekers and just can't wait. They insist on being seen first and thrust themselves to the front. Here are a few examples that have stuck in my mind over the years.

HELLO, DOLLY

I was giving a demonstration in Camberley one evening when I found the event suddenly taken over by a rather forceful lady. Some would call the behaviour she displayed assertive, others would call it downright rude. Whichever it was, it was certainly memorable.

I was in the middle of bringing another lady through at the time and was being drawn to a group of three middle-aged women who were sitting together. But before I could really get anywhere with that message, I became aware of a figure emerging to the right of these ladies, next to two gentlemen who were sitting a few rows back. This lady immediately took my attention away. She was clearly a 'queue jumper' and was in a hurry to get in touch with the audience.

I'd had a similar experience the last time I'd given a demonstration in Camberley so as I began to tune into this lady's energy, I couldn't help commenting on the impatience that seemed to be a hallmark of the town. 'This happened to me last time I was in this theatre,' I told the audience. 'People always jump the queue here. Is there something in the water here that makes people pushier?'

This produced a big laugh, of course, but I couldn't really hear it. All I could I hear was the song 'Hello, Dolly', really loudly in my head.

I was immediately drawn to the two men this lady had materialised next to. 'Excuse me, gents, do you understand the name Dolly or Dorothy?' I asked. 'Yes, my mother was called Dorothy,' one of them said, a little surprised. 'But everyone called her Dolly.' On hearing this, the woman threw out her arms and did a little curtsey, as if to say, 'Ta-dah, I'm here.' She was a real attention seeker.

As I say, I ordinarily expect spirits to stand behind me on the stage. So I asked this lady to join me. Again, it was obvious that she was a prima donna. She could have floated or just appeared on stage like most spirits would have done, but no, she had to make a big song and dance of it. I'm sure she thought that everyone in the theatre was watching her.

She was very, very dramatic, like an old-time actress, but her message was actually quite a sweet one. She had been very frail in her old age and had needed a great deal of looking after. She wanted to thank her son and his partner for being so patient and loving towards her. It had made her final days here in this life a much more bearable experience for her.

As the message drew to a close, I began to feel the most amazing sensation. It was as if I was wearing the best quality silk stockings money could buy. I could feel them on my legs.

At first I imagined these must have been stockings that Dolly wore, but I was soon seeing images of her son wearing them.

'I don't know what this means, but I am seeing you wearing silk stockings,' I said.

The son looked deeply embarrassed. 'Yes, that's right,' he said, producing howls of laughter from the audience.

It turned out that he was something of a drag queen in his private life and loved to dress up in women's underwear and stockings. Each to his own.

The message reminded me of a valuable lesson. Sometimes spirits are eager to come through because they have a hugely important, life-or-death message that they feel they have to get across. But at other times they simply want to express themselves – and be themselves. Dolly certainly did that.

JUMPING JANICE FLASH

Some spirits are absolutely desperate to make their presence felt. I have had communications from people within hours of them passing. Others are so eager to make a connection and let this world know that they have safely crossed over to the Other Side that they make their presence felt in quite dramatic fashion.

One of the more memorable examples of this was a lovely lady called Janice. I knew her through one of my most trusted assistants at my centre, Lucy, who had worked with her.

Janice was in her early fifties and had been diagnosed with an aggressive cancer. Within a few short months she had passed. I'd been away on tour when I'd heard the sad news. When I returned home a week or so later I'd assumed the funeral had taken place.

A few days later, Lucy and I travelled up to Norfolk to run a class for more than a dozen people. The moment we had begun the class we'd both picked up on an incredible energy that was virtually filling the room. Lucy immediately recognised it as the spirit of Janice. It was clear to me that hers was quite a chaotic energy, quite unruly.

We were there to help less experienced, developing mediums to practise their skills. So we asked a couple of them to try to interpret what Janice had to say. But it was incredibly difficult.

Both Lucy and I were able to see Janice. She was bouncing around the room like some hyperactive child. She was hopping onto the laps of different people in the circle, bouncing up and down and generally making a nuisance of herself.

It was impossible for our students to channel this energy. Even Lucy, who is pretty experienced too, was struggling to keep her friend under control. I decided that I'd have to take charge and told Janice to sit down. It wasn't easy. She had been quite a strong character, something of a bossy-boots, truth be told. So she didn't take kindly to it.

'Gosh, she was excited,' I said to the class, afterwards.

It was only on the drive back down from Norfolk that Lucy told me she was going to her funeral two days later.

'Funeral?' I said. 'I thought she'd been laid to rest last week.'

Apparently there had been some complication involving the hospital that had required a post-mortem. This world may have been taking its time, but, as one of the newest members of the spirit world, Janice had no intention of hanging around. It's rare that I've felt so much love, strength – and yes, bossiness – in a spirit. Her eagerness to prove that she'd made it safely across was incredible. Unsurprisingly, she kept popping up at sittings and circles that I ran at my centre for weeks afterwards. We were soon giving her a nickname: Jumping Janice Flash.

ONE NIGHT IN HEAVEN

The way in which people communicate from the Other Side can often reflect their personality. People who, for instance, loved music will often communicate to mediums in the form of songs or pieces of music to get their messages across. People who had a strong visual sense will tend to show images to communicate. Again, this underlines the fact that our essential self doesn't change on the Other Side. We remain the same personality, with the same character traits.

The experience the family of a young lady called Emily went through illustrates this rather beautifully.

Her passing affected me and my work colleagues quite deeply.

I first became aware of her one morning when I was teaching in Ireland. I got up with the distinct feeling that something wasn't quite right. I mentioned this over breakfast to my friend Lucy, with whom I was travelling. 'Something's wrong, I don't know what it is. But there's something,' I told her.

Within minutes I had got an urgent message from my son James, saying that my other son's girlfriend, Daisie, had just received some devastating news. Her cousin Emily had died the previous day. She was just eighteen. Emily was a very warm and loving young woman. She was quite artistic and loved music and dancing. She was full of life. Her loss had devastated her family and friends like Daisie.

From that moment on, she began to dominate the conversations and communications I had with the spirit world. I travelled back to England the following day to run my regular development classes. In the first of these, one of my students, a very new and inexperienced young woman, suddenly blurted out the name Emily in a really loud voice.

Her name kept recurring throughout the rest of the week.

She was buried on the Thursday. The following day I travelled out to Portugal where I was due to do a day of sittings with some friends. One or two of these friends knew Emily, and in particular her mother, Michelle, and one of them, a lady called Nicole, received a message from Emily while I was out there.

Another odd thing that happened was that I kept getting the image of sunflowers in my mind. The information came from a young girl, who was very gently communicating the image. I later spoke to Daisie, who told me that Emily's funeral had involved lots of sunflowers.

A short time later, I was lucky enough to meet her mother. Michelle told me the most beautiful story. She and her family had been watching a wonderful red sunset one evening. Emily had been a talented young artist with a real love for colour and design, and, as they looked at this gorgeous sunset, her foster brother, Braydon, took his mother by the arm and said: 'Emily has painted that for us.'

At that precise moment Michelle, Braydon and the rest of the family heard the sound of music coming from a large party room they have in their house. There was no one in the room. Somehow an iPod that was in there had come on and started playing a song. They recognised the music immediately. It was a favourite song of Emily's by M People, called 'One Night in Heaven'.

There's no question in my mind that it was their beloved daugther, communicating with them from the Afterlife through the things that she loved in this life.

Spirit Truth: your actions can't 'hold a spirit back'

There are so many mistruths and misconceptions about the spirit world, but to my mind one of the most annoying relates to how people should react when they lose a loved one. According to this 'theory', you shouldn't talk to or try to make any connection with your loved one after they pass over because it will somehow hold them back. Apparently it 'holds them back from the light'. Whenever I hear this I get extremely annoyed because it actually compounds rather than lessens the grief of those who are suffering.

I've known people who have taken this misconception to heart and become cold and completely cut off from their loved one. They have taken down photographs and memorabilia. They have expunged their home of all evidence of the person with whom they used to share it. Almost always they have done this against their better instincts. They would have been better off listening to those instincts because the truth is none of us can hold back the spirits of our loved ones from anything. And as for the idea that they are somehow being denied 'the light', this is absolute codswallop – they have passed over, they are in the light already.

GOOD NIGHT, DARLING

Whenever I hear someone mention this sort of behaviour I tell them the same thing: they may want the best for themselves and their loved ones in spirit, but all they are doing is enhancing the grief and suffering, on both sides.

The case of a lady I saw a year or so ago illustrates this perfectly.

One Monday morning, I arrived in the reception of my centre to be greeted by a beautiful, elderly lady who had booked herself in for a sitting with me. She must have been an incredible beauty in her prime. She could still have been a model – and maybe even was. I will call her Jessica.

There was a sadness about Jessica's face, however. As the sitting got under way I began to understand what was causing it. I was soon sensing the energy of an elderly man. He was a handsome creature too and was still quite dashing even though he'd passed in his early eighties. It was clear that this was her husband. I will call him Ronald.

Ronald showed me a succession of images which made it obvious the pair had enjoyed an absolutely wonderful life together. They had been married when they were in their twenties and had remained happily together for almost sixty years. I glimpsed them on holidays, dancing and sitting in their garden together. They seemed a truly golden couple.

As the sitting progressed, I sensed that Ronald had passed from a stroke just a few months earlier. It was an instantaneous passing; he had had no chance to say goodbye to Jessica or anyone else, for that matter. As his energy grew and I felt him draw closer to me, I sensed that Ronald was rather emotional and upset. He was upset that he had passed within a few months short of their golden wedding anniversary. They had already started making plans for a big, family celebration and it had really hurt him to see Jessica and their children cancelling everything after his funeral.

But it was something else that was upsetting him even more than this.

'He is telling me that you said goodnight to each other every night of your marriage,' I said. 'Even if one of you was staying somewhere else, you would call each other at bedtime.'

She smiled and nodded at this. 'That's true,' she said.

'He's really upset because you don't do that any more,' I said.

Jessica looked shocked and a little shaken by this. 'Well, I'd love to say goodnight to him every night. And inside I am desperate to do so every night before I go to sleep. But I've been told that by talking to those who have passed over you hold them back,' she said.

For a moment I had to hold my tongue. But then I gathered myself and told Jessica that she was mistaken and that she mustn't carry on ignoring Ronald like this. She was absolutely elated to hear this. She couldn't thank me enough for taking this weight from her shoulders.

I have absolutely no doubt that she went back home and had a long and heartfelt chat with her late husband when she went to bed that night. And I'm certain that she will keep saying goodnight to him until the day comes when they are reunited once more on the Other Side.

Spirit Truth: **spirit connects with us all in different ways**

People often think they are incapable of connecting with spirit. They imagine that it's an experience that's only available to mediums. That's simply not true.

Spirits are energy and everyone can feel energy. Just think about it for a second. We can all walk into a room and feel whether the atmosphere is positive or negative, whether the mood is up or down. There's not a huge difference between doing this and being able to feel our spirit families around us.

What's interesting is that each of us will feel that spirit in a different way. I recently read for a mother and daughter who connected with the recently passed spirit of their husband and father. He was a very well adjusted spirit even though he had not long crossed over. His energy was very strong and made its presence felt in the room. But that presence manifested itself in different ways for the two women in his life.

The daughter was able to physically feel him tapping her on the head. But the wife couldn't feel him. She could smell him. She had a different way of connecting with him.

Afterwards the lady asked me why this was. I told her that she was actually too close to him physically to be able to feel him yet. She had been with him for more than forty years. When you spend that much time with someone you almost become one. You even finish each other's sentences. You become like one soul. So you can't feel your own energy.

I'd seen the same thing in mothers who had lost their child, especially when they were young. I don't mean to dismiss a father's grief, but because a child has physically grown inside their mother, they are part of who and what that child is. That's a wonderful thing, of course. But the downside is that it is more difficult for the mother whose child has been lost to feel that child than it is for the father.

Spirit Truth: sometimes spirits are there for other reasons than to communicate with us

---

Spirits don't always materialise in order to communicate with us. Sometimes they are there for other reasons – perhaps to make sure all is well, to help another spirit, or simply because they are curious. I've encountered many such spirits. Here are a few memorable examples.

BRING ME SUNSHINE

One evening a year or two ago, I was demonstrating at a new venue, one I'd not worked at before – Harpenden's Public Halls. I work in so many different venues, up and down the country, that one blends into another after a while. Obviously venues like the Hammersmith Apollo, where I performed as one of the Three Mediums, stick in the mind. But often it's simply a question of arriving at the stage door, going into my dressing room, going out on stage, meeting people afterwards then heading either back to the hotel or home. At least Harpenden was relatively close to my home and, as I stepped onto the stage, I knew that I'd be back in my own bed by midnight.

It was an enjoyable demonstration and a warm and receptive audience, which always helps. As the evening unfolded, however, the most noticeable thing was not so much the spirits that were talking to me, but the one that was not.

From the moment I began the demonstration, I was aware of a man who was standing in the wings of the stage area, to my left. He was watching me and my act very carefully. He was clearly taking everything in. There was no real expression on his face, however. Every time I looked round he just looked at me. But he wouldn't come forward at all and whenever I tried to make eye contact with him, he would look away.

I assumed that he was there to make contact with someone and that I'd work out the identity of the audience member he was trying to connect with before the end of the evening. But the longer the demonstration went on, the more obvious it was that he wasn't interested in communicating with me.

As the evening began drawing to a close, I was a little bit concerned that I had someone's father or brother or husband here and that they were missing out on a message of some kind. So towards the end I asked the audience for their help in identifying him.

'I just wanted to tell you all that there's been a man standing here all night watching me. He's made no attempt to communicate. I think he's just here to see what's going on,' I joked. Just in case anyone recognised him, I then went on to describe him. 'He's tall, slim, slightly balding and is wearing thick spectacles. His suit jacket looks like it's a bit too big for him.'

It was then that it occurred to me who he reminded me of. 'He looks just like Eric Morecambe. I half expect him to break into "Bring Me Sunshine" at any moment,' I said, drawing laughter from the audience. I looked across at the man to see if this had at least drawn a smile from him, but again he looked away the instant I tried to make eye contact.

The description didn't seem to register with anyone in the audience so I just told them that if he did sound familiar they should come and talk to me afterwards when I was signing books and autographs in the foyer of the halls.

I didn't really think anything more about it. But the moment the curtain came down and I left the stage, a member of the crew, Michael, came running up to me.

'Tracy, that bloke who was standing at the side of the stage, what did he look like again?' he said.

Crew aren't supposed to accept messages during my demonstrations, for obvious reasons. People will only think it's a plant or a fix of some kind. So I assumed that the man sounded familiar to him and thought the message might be for him.

'As I said, he's tall, a bit gangly, with thick, National Health spectacles, like Eric Morecambe. Do you know him?' I asked.

Michael just looked at me a bit quizzically, as if he was trying to work out if I was having a laugh or something. 'Have you ever been here before?' he said.

'No,' I said.

'OK, come with me,' he said.

So he led me from the dressing room out into the foyer of the theatre, where I was going to be doing some signing in a few minutes' time. Behind the table there was a massive portrait of Eric Morecambe, one half of Britain's best-loved double act Morecambe and Wise.

'Why's that there?' I said, slightly taken aback.

'Because the Harpenden Public Halls is made up of two parts. One is called the Southdown Room and the other one is known as the Eric Morecambe Theatre. He used to live near here and was a big supporter of this place.'

He must have thought I was an idiot, because I didn't know that. As I said, I play in so many venues that I tend to whizz in through the stage door and leave the same way a few hours later without having paid any attention to my surroundings.

Suddenly it all made sense. I had to laugh at myself. I'd been really concerned that the man was somebody's loved one and I'd somehow missed the message that he was there to deliver. But it wasn't that at all. He was obviously just hanging around watching me. It wasn't being done in a negative way at all. It was as if he was part of the crew. He was watching another professional.

Every now and again something happens to me that leaves me feeling quietly glowing inside. That was one such occasion. I was amazed. When I was growing up, Eric Morecambe had been a huge figure in our household. Like most other families at the time, we would be glued to the television whenever the 'Morecambe & Wise Show' came on, especially on Christmas Day. I thought it was very cool that I'd spent an evening entertaining one of the finest comedians and entertainers that this country has ever produced. It put a real spring in my step as I headed home that night. I hummed 'Bring Me Sunshine' in the car all the way.

FATHER TED

The scene that unfolded one night on the stage of the Helix theatre in Dublin could have come straight out of the television comedy series 'Father Ted'.

Midway through the demonstration I was on stage with my colleague and good friend Colin Fry when I became aware of a nun walking up and down the aisles of the theatre. She looked like a very stern and strict Sister. You really wouldn't have wanted to mess with her. 'I wonder what she's got to say for herself?' I asked myself as she made her way up to the stage and stood beside me.

As it turned out, she didn't want to say anything. When I tried to engage her in some kind of conversation, she just kept shaking her head disapprovingly and nodding towards Colin. When I turned, I nearly jumped out of my skin. Standing between me and Colin was a priest, in full regalia.

It was he who brought to mind Father Ted.

The evidence I get sometimes consists of smells that are familiar from my own life. On this occasion, all I could smell was whiskey – Jameson's, I think. It immediately took me back to my childhood, in a family with a strong Catholic tradition. While I was growing up, whenever we had a confirmation for one of my cousins there was always a priest sitting in the corner who had had one too many. This priest reminded me of the old, drunken priest who sits in Father Ted's living room, letting loose a string of swear words every now and again.

The message he had to pass on was actually quite touching. He was trying to get in contact with a lady who was in the audience. It turned out she was a member of what was, in effect, his second family. This lady's parents had been very hospitable and Christian people, who had always provided the priest with Sunday lunch and a drink after the church service each weekend. But he had led a lonely and isolated life and had died that way as well. He showed me an image of him riding a bicycle along a windy cliff edge in the countryside outside Dublin. He had gone over the edge and died when he hit the rocks far below.

His message was about how grateful he was to this family for the kindness and support they'd shown him when he was alive. He obviously didn't have a wife and children of his own and these people had become a kind of surrogate family to him. It was a bittersweet message. On the one hand, the scene on the stage was like something out of a comedy sketch. But the message itself was very poignant.

Throughout the message, the nun had stood to my side, watching me like a hawk. But as soon as the priest had delivered his message and disappeared, she was ready to go too. As she left she gave me another look, this time a lot friendlier. It was as if she was saying thank you. Once again, it was evidence that we shouldn't always expect the spirit world to speak to us. Sometimes, as in the case of this nun, they are here for a very different reason.

Spirit Truth: haunted houses, poltergeists and ghosts are myths

---

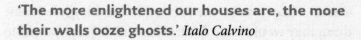

'The more enlightened our houses are, the more their walls ooze ghosts.' *Italo Calvino*

Another misconception that really annoys me concerns ghosts, poltergeists and so-called 'haunted houses'. According to a lot of people, many of whom have a vested interest in encouraging people to believe what they are saying, these spirits are all troubled souls who are somehow 'trapped'. They also appear only at night when they are certain to scare anyone who catches a glimpse of them.

That is, I'm afraid, complete rubbish. Yes, there are spirits who spend their time in certain locations and are more visible there than they might be elsewhere. Some of these locations also happen to be old buildings with a long association with human energy. It's only logical that they would be in these places, especially when mediums or paranormal investigators go looking for them. There are two main reasons for this.

Firstly, the spirit world is always going gather when mediums visit a particular space. It's the same when a client comes and sits in my consulting room. The spirits will know that that is where that particular person will be at that particular moment and they will take advantage of the fact that person is with a medium. If I were to go to a haunted castle, they would know that I was coming. So I could almost 100 per cent guarantee that I would find the spirit of someone there. But that person wouldn't be stuck. That person wouldn't be trapped in between two worlds. That person would simply be doing the same thing they would have done in this life if they wanted to talk to the Other Side: they would seek out a medium.

Secondly, spirits, like you and I living in this world, are drawn to a particular place because they want to be there. In this respect, again, they are behaving no differently to the way any of us behave day in day out. We all like to hang out in the places that make us comfortable, that we like to call home. Just because they have passed to spirit this hasn't changed.

During the course of my career, I've met many people who have changed their attitude completely once they've understood these simple principles. One example that sticks in my mind was a guy who had been to a supposedly famously haunted castle, Chillingham Castle in Northumberland. I met him at a party and he immediately made a beeline for me. He told me that every time he had been to this place he had heard a baby crying.

'It's obvious that this baby must have been murdered or incarcerated there and is still in pain even though it has passed over,' he told me, seemingly very excited at his 'discovery'.

I just looked at him and shook my head in disbelief.

'Why is that obvious? Why is the fact that a baby is crying proof that it must have been murdered? That makes absolutely no sense,' I told him.

He just looked at me as if I'd told him Father Christmas wasn't real. So I spelled it out in clearer detail for him.

'Look at it this way. In the physical world, my babies used to cry all the time. It didn't mean that I was trying to murder them. They simply wanted my attention, they wanted my love,' I said.

By now he was non-plussed.

'Did the baby at Chillingham stop crying? Yes, it did? So did it not occur to you that it might be that its spirit mother or another relative had heard its cries and had arrived to comfort it in the same way that it would get comfort here in this world?'

'Hmmm, I'd never thought about it like that before,' he said eventually. He then slunk off, looking rather deflated.

This is what irritates me about the whole 'most haunted/ghost hunting' industry. It's a very lucrative one, as anyone who watches some of the specialist cable television channels will know. But it always jumps to the worst conclusions. When people go on a ghost hunt they are looking for the morbid and for the tragic. Which is not the case in most instances. Spirits are simply existing in the spaces that make them feel safe and secure and comfortable. If you have a favourite space, whether it's a favourite room, chair or house, why wouldn't you come back and bring your energy there when you pass over? It's always got to be the worst thing – a child has died at birth or has been murdered and buried in the garden. Why? Why does that have to be the case?

Why wouldn't the 'ghost of the grey lady' that seems to be so common everywhere be someone who is very proud of her garden that she is walking around? Mightn't she want to be showing you this wonderful piece of greenery that she's very proud of? Why does she need to be crying all the time? I'm always glad to be able to get this message across to people.

THE IDEAL WOMAN

I travel fairly widely these days, appearing in demonstrations and holding sittings for people around Europe. It was during one trip, to Portugal, that I encountered a lady who was having a particular problem with a spirit that seemed to have taken up residence in her house.

This lady was actually English and her name was Barbara. She was staying in Portugal for a while on holiday but was based in Epping. She admitted to me that she was in no hurry to get back to her house because, as she put it, she had a 'spirit stalker' there.

Barbara explained to me that she and her husband had bought the house quite recently. It was a very grand, historic house on the edge of Epping Forest. It had stood there for centuries and had a rich and fascinating history. Unfortunately for Barbara, that history had attracted this particular spirit to spend time there. Barbara told me that it was as if this 'ghost' was following her around the house.

I agreed to hold a sitting for her in which I'd try to explore with spirit what was going on back in Epping.

Now an excitable medium would have immediately concluded that Barbara was being haunted by this spirit. But I soon worked out that this was far from the truth.

The spirit was clearly that of a man. At one point I picked up on the name William, which I subsequently found was interesting because William Shakespeare had apparently spent some time there at one point in his life.

During the sitting, I could feel the man's presence – and the effect he was having upon Barbara. As I focused on the energy within this house, I could hear all the door latches being closed. Barbara nodded vigorously at this and said she kept hearing that sound. For her it was quite an uncomfortable experience, but to me it sounded like he was closing the doors to make sure that she was safe.

The more I learned about this man, the more convinced I was that he was a totally benign influence in the house.

I got the strong feeling, for instance, that he hadn't enjoyed a happy marriage or a happy home life. Barbara's home was, I knew from friends' accounts, a fabulously happy place. She was a great cook, homemaker and entertainer. She was also a great wife and a loving mother to her four sons.

I had the very strong feeling that this man was simply attracted to her energy. He enjoyed being around her and being in the home that she had created. 'As far as he's concerned, you're his ideal woman,' I told her.

Barbara took some consolation from this, but was still uncomfortable about going back to the house. So

I agreed to make contact with the man and explain her feelings to him. I asked Barbara to put out the same message when she got home.

We dealt with it very easily. He'd soon moved on, leaving Barbara in peace. My main point here is that this was a problem that didn't require any great drama.

I've been called to so many homes or buildings that are supposed to be haunted. I'm sure people expect me to start behaving like someone out of *The Exorcist* and blessing the place with holy water. But the bottom line is usually the same as it was in this case: it's simply a spirit occupying a place where it feels happy and comfortable. Some people are disappointed when I tell them this, but the truth is that spirits get blamed for far too much. Most of the time we should simply leave them in peace.

Spirit Truth: poltergeists are simply spirits in need of your attention

---

As well as ghosts, of course, people also get obsessed with so-called violent spirits, or poltergeists. I'm often asked what I think about this phenomenon and I always answer the same way.

To me a poltergeist is simply a spirit that is trying to get your attention. Again, there's nothing unusual about this. Spirits are a little bit like two-year-olds. If they want your attention they will do whatever they need to do in order to get it. So if you are in the room with them but ignoring them, they may well make a big noise or flash a light or switch the television off. It's a way of catching your attention.

If you think about it, it's probably very frustrating for them, especially if you have invited them in, which people often do when they are in search of a message or some kind of sign of the Afterlife. They may begin gently, perhaps by flashing a light or ringing a doorbell. If the reaction to that is disbelief or disinterest then they are going to try even harder to catch your eye. However, we shouldn't think of this as malicious. If something gets broken it's accidental because it's a heightened build-up of energy.

Again too many people like to think the negative, not the positive when it comes to poltergeists. It's quite sad really. Ultimately, they are simply the spirits of people trying to say they are OK, trying to say that they are around, but who are being ignored and treated negatively. It's like inviting a friend into your home, then going to sleep on the sofa as they try to talk to you. You should behave towards them as you would towards a human being that is physically here. You shouldn't play with their emotions and energy. Treat them with the respect they deserve.

PART THREE:
The Truth about Mediums

'One sees clearly only with the heart.
Anything essential is invisible to the eyes.'
Antoine de Saint-Exupéry

There are so many misconceptions about mediums and mediumship. People have all sorts of ideas about who we are, how we acquire our knowledge, the way we work and how we communicate with spirit. So I'd like to take this opportunity to answer a few of the most common questions I get asked during the course of my work.

Spirit Truth: (almost) anyone can be a medium

There are all sorts of stereotypes about mediums. A lot of people expect us to be colourful showmen and women with a talent for turning the art of communicating with the Other Side into an entertainment. Others expect us to be very pious, religious people. The truth, of course, is that like every other profession, we mediums come in all shapes and sizes, ages and colours. There are no rules and regulations, especially as far as I'm concerned. So absolutely anyone can become a medium, provided – that is – you have a few qualities.

The first is that you are psychic. It's an inescapable fact that not all psychics are mediums, but all mediums are psychic.

If I am invited to teach a class of advanced mediums, I will often ask, 'How many of you are psychic?' Usually a few will put their hand up so I will tell them, 'The rest of you can go home then.' That's because if you cannot feel a living person, which is what a psychic does, then you are never going to feel a spirit person. Psychics work with the soul, but mediums work with the souls of those who have passed. Psychics blend with the soul of the present, whereas mediums blend with the souls of the past.

Another requirement is the ability to connect from the heart.

During the course of my career, I've seen all sorts of people become mediums. One of the least likely is a young guy called Ryan who trained with me at my centre. Ryan was about twenty-nine and a builder. He was a young dad with two kids. His approach to mediumship was very straightforward. He would simply stand up and just pass on whatever it was he was getting. There were no airs and graces. His messages were very raw, but – to me – that is the essence of mediumship. It has to come from the heart. Whatever you say doesn't need to make sense to you, it only needs to make sense to the person who is receiving the message.

Prior to joining my circle, Ryan had been to various other places that had all sorts of rules and regulations. He was once told he would have to sit in a circle for four years, for instance. They simply didn't know what to do with him. I have no doubt that Ryan is a raw talent and he is going to go on to do amazing things. And that's because he represents the purity of mediumship. He tells it from the heart.

One other quality that is essential, as far as I am concerned, is honesty.

Honesty is an obsession of mine, possibly an unhealthy one. I have this idea in my head that if I don't tell the truth, I will land in the spirit world in a plane. It will be like that scene from the movie *Airplane* where everyone is slapping that lady, stopping her getting off the plane. I won't be allowed in the spirit world.

So I am always honest with everyone, regardless of the consequences. If, for instance, I'm being told that someone has a health problem I have to pass that information on. Recently, for example, I told a woman who had terminal cancer that she would be here for Christmas but wouldn't be here for New Year. She wanted to know her time frame, so I asked the questions for her.

And she died on December 28. Spirit came straight to me and told me.

This may seem harsh, but I always say to people, 'If you don't want the truth, then don't ask me.' Sometimes our job as psychic mediums is to empower people by telling the truth.

I met a lady once whose husband had terminal cancer. The message to her was that spirit was very cross with her. She wasn't letting him go out, she wasn't letting him see friends or do anything, because he was dying of cancer. Their message was that she needed to let him out. He needed to live the rest of his life, not live in this controlled situation. She was not allowing him to live.

I didn't consider that bad news to pass on. It's a question of perception really. One person's bad news is another person's good news. Many people might consider that mean of me. But by the end of the sitting she had realised that I was absolutely right. She had been looking at it from her own perspective – wanting to protect her husband. Her husband just wanted to be free to live the rest of his days.

Spirit Truth: the truth is positive – always

I have to be truthful with people like this all the time. In a previous book I wrote about an eighty-four-year-old man who came to see me and I was told that he needed to go to hospital for a heart operation – immediately. He went back to his workplace and duly collapsed. He had the operation and pulled through. He later came back to thank me for telling him what he needed to do.

Now from some people's perspective, again, I was giving him bad news. But if I hadn't given him that news, it would have been much worse news for him and his family. The same thing applied with a lady whom I told to postpone her plans to move from London to a home in the countryside in Dorset. I told her she should leave it for six months because her mother had a serious problem with her chest and needed attention. That woman trusted me and didn't move. She got her mum to hospital where it turned out she had lung cancer. Her mother passed six months later.

Now, if she'd moved to Dorset she'd have been miles from her mother and she wouldn't have been able to spend time with her. Was I wrong to give her that news, or was I right? I feel I had to; I had to tell her the truth.

I apply this principle on a daily basis. If I am connecting a man and the widow to whom he was married for fifty years before his unexpected passing, I am not going to tell her that he is happy on the Other Side. I won't say that he's desperately sad or depressed, but at the same time I can't say he's happy. I can't tell someone who has been living with the same partner for forty-odd years of solid marriage that her husband has died and is now happy in the spirit world because he has been taken away from her. Would you be happy if you were taken away from your husband or wife like that? Especially if it happened quickly and they had not been given time to prepare. If I say that someone has passed into the spirit world and is happy as Larry, having the time of his life up there, how is that going to make the other person feel? They are going to start thinking, 'Oh, didn't he love me?' and 'Was he desperate to get away from me?' The truth is that neither side is happy and they are both getting on with it until they are reunited on the Other Side.

I don't consider that to be negative. It's not a negative, it's the truth. And sometimes the truth is a positive.

Spirit Truth: there are no secrets in the spirit world

Unfortunately, the truth can often be uncomfortable. I often find myself in the position of having told people things that they have not wanted to hear. It can be inconvenient – and even upsetting, at times. But my view – and, more importantly, the view of spirit – is that unless you know the truth, you aren't going to be able to get on with the rest of your life here. So I make no apologies for being 100 per cent truthful.

Of course, it's a two-way street. I've heard things from spirit that I've not wanted to hear. But that comes with the territory; I understand that now, partly from personal experience.

One experience, in particular, illustrated this. It happened a few years ago when I went to see an amazing medium called Evelyn Lloyd. She was a remarkable woman, who didn't become a medium until very late in her life. She worked from the age of seventy-eight until she died in her nineties. She hadn't been allowed to do work when her husband was alive, but then when he passed he came back to her and told her to get on with it.

As a young, up-and-coming medium, I learned a lot from Evelyn when I attended a couple of workshops that she held. She was an inspirational figure and even came through with my Pops during one demonstration. It was so clearly him, he even had a pigeon on his shoulder.

And she gave me a lot of really invaluable advice. For instance, she was the person who told me not to listen to those more traditional mediums who argued that all mediums needed to work consistently through spirit guides. She saw that I took a more direct approach and encouraged me to do that, to just work with spirit if that was the way I felt.

Because I was such an admirer of Evelyn I took my entire circle along to see her one evening. What nobody knew at that time was that I was going through something of an upheaval in my professional and personal life. I had been looking for a new studio and had been looking at a particular property. I had also begun dating someone new. I didn't particularly want to share either of these pieces of news so had deliberately kept quiet about them. It didn't stay that way for long, however.

Evelyn began the demonstration and quickly began passing on information that was clearly related to me. 'I can see a good-looking man on a motorbike,' she said. 'His surname is Smith.'

I couldn't help blurting out a word of protest. 'Excuse me, that's a secret,' I said.

She then described seeing me looking at my new potential studio. 'You are not sure whether it is the right place for you to base your business,' she said. Again it was something that my friends didn't know anything about.

She could tell that I was cheesed off at having two secrets aired in public. But then she said something I'll never forget. 'You can't pick and choose what you hear when you communicate with spirit. And there are no such things as secrets,' she said.

I was absolutely gobsmacked. But it taught me an important lesson. She was right – there are no such things as secrets in the spirit world. It's a truth I have seen illustrated many times since then.

THE PREGNANT PAUSE

It's my belief that if I'm given something by spirit, I am allowed to share it. I will control the way I pass it on, I am very careful. But I strongly believe that if I am shown something it is for a reason. And it's my duty as a medium to get that information to the person who needs to hear it, whatever the consequences.

Of course, honesty isn't always the safest policy. It can get you into trouble, as it almost did one night when I was demonstrating early in my career at a large theatre in Liverpool. It was a big, scary venue with two and a half thousand people there. I was still quite new so was doing fifteen-minute slots. I was in the process of giving a message to a family who were sitting in the front row of the balcony. There were five women, all with the same dark hair and striking looks. I could tell immediately they were a very tight-knit tribe.

The spirit trying to connect with them was the matriarch of the family, the mother of the older women and the nan of the younger women in the party. She was a very strong lady, as indeed were her relatives.

It took me a while to get through to them properly. Everything I said to them brought a firm shake of the head and a firm 'no'. For a moment or two I was a bit thrown by this and even wondered whether I had the right people. But there was no doubt it was the female head of this family. I just had to get to the nitty-gritty to convince them that it was her.

After a couple of minutes I began to see a new image forming. I recognised it immediately. It was a scan for a baby. I also recognised that it might represent a secret for some members of the family.

'Your nan is sending one of you congratulations,' I said.

Again there was a nonplussed look and a mildly aggressive 'no' from the five of them.

'She's congratulating the one who is pregnant,' I continued.

That brought a really strong reaction. There was a lot of glancing up and down the line, looking at each other, and a lot of arm-crossing and head-shaking. 'No, no, no,' they kept saying.

I totally believe in spirit and I know I'm not going to be told untruths, so I had to be firm with them. 'Well, I can definitely tell you that one of you is pregnant,' I said. 'Hold on, I'll just ask Nan to tell me which one of you it is.'

I was immediately given the number four.

'It's the fourth one along, you are pregnant.'

Well, you could have cut the atmosphere in the theatre with a knife. The fourth member of the party, a pretty young women probably in her early twenties, sat there motionless, saying nothing while the others looked at her.

I knew I was right and was soon given another little piece of information. 'Oh, sorry, apparently the bloke doesn't know yet either, does he?' I said.

At that point, the girl covered her face with her hands. She then said: 'No, I haven't told anybody.'

The whole audience roared. From the looks her relatives were giving her, I could tell that this was going to mean trouble for the young lady. But I had no regrets. Spirit needed to get that message across, and it was my job to achieve this. I couldn't let the consequences affect me.

Spirit Truth: **mediums can get taken over by spirits**

A lot of people are fascinated by what goes on physically and mentally when I am in contact with the spirit world. 'Do you feel or look different when spirit is with you?' some ask me.

The truth is that it varies according to the kind of connection I'm making, as well as the personality of the spirit in question. Most of the time, I simply see images and hear thoughts that give me an idea of what is being communicated. But there are times when I do get taken over by spirit to some extent.

People close to me often say that they see a big change in me during the hour or so before a demonstration. Apparently my eyes change colour and I become a slightly different person, as if I'm taking on a spirit personality. I've come to realise that this is because spirits are blending with me before I communicate with them fully.

As you might expect, this can be a strange and unsettling experience for me. There are times when it's also a little bit inconvenient. I remember once I was driving to a demonstration and found myself acting in a really aggressive manner, as if I was some white van driver exhibiting a bad case of road rage. I was cursing and swearing and waving my arms at everyone that I imagined was slowing me down or being disrespectful to me on the road.

When I got to the demonstration, however, I realised that it wasn't me behaving like this. The first spirit that I was connecting with that evening was a really aggressive and feisty old guy who wanted to pass on a message about how he was still angry on the Other Side. Afterwards I felt like finding every single person I'd abused on the road and apologising to them personally.

A SENSE OF PEACE

There are also times when the close encounters with spirit can become very confusing.

The most memorable example of this I have experienced happened one late summer morning a couple of years ago when I was driving to my centre to do some one-to-one sessions. As I sat at the wheel of my car I was suddenly aware of a really uncomfortable feeling. Soon I felt a really strong sensation that I was unwell.

There was no warning. I was suddenly overcome by real panic. I began to see vivid images of me in hospital and undergoing treatment. Within moments I was convinced I had cancer.

It was completely illogical. I'd been experiencing a

few unusual pains and intended to get to the doctor. But there was no cause to think I had anything serious. Logic didn't have anything to do with it, however. The wave of emotions that were now flowing through me were so intense that I had to pull over into a lay-by. I sat there and burst into floods of tears.

'I can't go to work in this state,' I said to myself. So I called Daisie who worked with me and told her that I'd not be able to do any sittings that morning. I blurted out something about me having cancer and needing to go to the doctor. It probably sounded completely unhinged.

Fortunately Daisie is quite a sensible girl and talked me down. 'Tracy, just come in and sit down for a bit, we will make you a cup of tea and talk about it,' she said. 'If you need to cancel the appointments and go to the doctor, we can do it then. But just get yourself here in one piece and let's talk about it.'

She then added something that pulled me back to reality. 'And Tracy, you have to remember sometimes that it's not you, it's them. This might be spirit sending you a message about someone else, not you.'

I realised she was right. So I pulled myself together, got back on the road and headed in.

By the time I go to the centre I was a few minutes late. My first client was there waiting for me. Her name was Avril. She was a really beautiful lady, immaculately turned-out and very polite and proper. I apologised for my lateness and took her through.

By now I'd put the experience in the car to the back

of my mind. The minute I sat down with her, however, I began to sense the same feelings I'd experienced minutes earlier.

We were soon in the presence of an elderly lady. I sensed it was Avril's mother and gave her some information which confirmed this. The mother then began to show me images of Avril in hospital. Immediately, a thought began to crystallize in my mind.

'You've come out of hospital today, haven't you?' I said.

'That's right,' she nodded.

'You've got terminal cancer, haven't you?' I asked.

'Yes, that's right,' she said.

I was stunned and would probably have burst into tears if Avril hadn't been so composed and calm about the situation. 'Please carry on,' she said, sensing my discomfort.

Her mother began explaining to me that Avril was worried about what was going to happen when she passed away. So, through me, she reassured her that she didn't need to worry about the children, that everything would be OK and that her husband and family would cope.

By the end of the sitting, Avril was dabbing away the tears. But I was incredibly moved by the dignity and control she showed. It was, as you can imagine, an extremely emotional sitting. Afterwards, however, as we chatted over a cup of tea, Avril told me that the sitting had been a huge help to her.

'It's given me a sense of peace,' she said. 'I now know where I'm going, and who is going to be there. And I know my children and my husband are going to be fine as well. So thank you very much.'

That evening, as I took stock of what had happened during the day, I realised what had happened. I had been picking up all those feelings from spirit on the way into work. Spirit had got so close to me that it had become part of me. It was an object lesson for me.

It was around five months later that the full significance of the sitting made itself clear.

I am always very clear that I don't want any advance information about people before they come in for a sitting. I don't want to be accused of cheating. More importantly, I don't want to confuse or over-complicate my connection with spirit.

So when a young woman sat down and I began to communicate with a slightly older person, I knew nothing about who she – or the spirit – was. She received a communication from her sister, who had passed very recently. As we chatted afterwards, the lady asked me if I wanted to know who we'd been connecting with.

'Do you want me to tell you?' she wondered.

'If you like,' I said, even though I had my suspicions.

'You read for my sister Avril a few months ago. Three months after you read for her she passed over,' she said. 'She told us that you had given her an important message that had helped her deal with what was about to happen to her. It was a huge comfort. It meant that she wasn't afraid to die.'

I got quite emotional about this. The thought that I had taken the fear of death away from her sister was overwhelming to me. It's what my job is all about.

KEEPING ME ON MY TOES

The spirit world is always unpredictable. You never, ever know what to expect. For that reason, my motto is expect the unexpected. But even then I am surprised by what I encounter at times.

Nothing surprised me – and freaked me out – more than a message I received when I was demonstrating at the Harlow Playhouse quite recently. I was really excited about working there because I'd never demonstrated there before. I had a lot of family and friends supporting me there that night. Perhaps as a result of this, the energy was really, really high. That, in turn, may well have contributed to the extraordinary message that came through that night.

Something that often causes people to raise their eyebrows a little is the fact that I normally take my shoes off when I'm working. I am, if you like, the Sandie Shaw of mediumship, the barefoot medium. It doesn't normally have any impact on my mediumship, but tonight was different. As I announced that I was about to connect with the last message of the night, I began to feel a really strange sensation in my feet. I immediately found myself being super-conscious of them, something that normally doesn't happen.

The spirit coming through was a father who was giving a message to his daughter Carly, who was in the front row. He was a really friendly, bubbly dad. It was clear from the outset that he loved his daughter and was overjoyed to be reunited with her from spirit.

The further I got with this message, however, the weirder my feet began to feel. By now I'd somehow wandered to the very front of the stage, where it dropped down to the floor below. I found myself kneeling down there. It was no easy feat to pull off considering I was wearing a full evening gown, I can tell you.

It was obvious spirit was making me do this. So I began to focus on my feet in an attempt to work out what it was trying to tell me. As I did so the feeling in my legs changed once more. This time I now felt as if I didn't have any legs at all. I then started to see some images in my head. I will never forget them.

All I could I see was someone cutting this man's toes off. And I mean cutting off his toes, not his toenails. Someone was using a hacksaw to do the job. It was really a gruesome, disgusting sight, to be honest, even though – thankfully – I couldn't see any blood or gristle or anything like that. At one point I began to wonder whether I might be sick on stage.

Now you might have imagined that this message would have upset the recipient, but Carly wasn't in distress at all. In fact, she was laughing. I was baffled so asked for her help to understand.

It turned out that as an elderly man, her father had lost his leg and had it replaced with a wooden one. The process of fitting the wooden leg had been tricky, however. The leg that had been made for him didn't fit his shoe. As a result of this, someone had sawn the toes off this wooden leg.

'We always used to joke that he had a foot with no toes,' Carly smiled.

I spoke to her briefly afterwards and she thanked me for giving her such amazingly accurate evidence. I was pleased, despite the fact that it had almost made me sick! My goal as a medium is to bring through the best evidence possible so as to convince people that I really am in contact with their loved ones.

Too many people are regurgitating mediums. They all do the same thing. And that's not what I want to do. I want to be made to work hard like that, because I want people to come to my evenings and not go home having seen the same sort of thing they could see anywhere. As I headed home myself that night, I was pretty certain that was the case!

Spirit Truth: sometimes spirits practise tough love

An accusation that is made against the spirit world sometimes is that the spirits don't care. I'm often approached by people at the end of a demonstration who tell me that they are convinced the spirits of loved ones who have passed over 'don't care' what is happening to them in this world.

They will come up to me and tell me that their marriage has collapsed, they've become ill or they've lost their job, but haven't heard anything from their mother, father, wife, husband or whoever. They will say things like: 'If they really loved me they would have contacted me through someone like you' or 'It's their fault that my life has fallen apart.' This makes no sense. For instance, if your mother were alive, would you blame her for the fact that your wife is having an affair with another man? Of course you wouldn't.

I compare the spirits' attitude to watching a toddler running down a hill. You know that your child is going to fall over, maybe graze his knees or bump his head and start crying. But you let them do it because you know that's the only way to learn. It's the same if a spirit is watching over someone who is heading down a path that is – in the long term – going to teach them something worthwhile or lead them to a better place in their life. But if they can say something that will help you, they will.

There's a real, true-grit honesty about the spirit world. It isn't tied up in all the fakery and lies of this world. Spirits make contact with us to empower us and tell us the truth. So there's no point in them contacting us to soothe our egos and tell us lies, even if they could do that. That would hurt us more in the long term. Whether you like it or not, they are going to tell you the truth.

But equally there are times when they know it is necessary for them to stand back and let things take their natural course. They know that is the best way for them to fulfil their purpose.

I know this is the case myself. During the course of my life, I have had to make mistakes in order to learn. Goodness knows I've made enough of them. The spirit world could have led me away from some of those mistakes. But it knew better, it knew that I was only going to develop and head down the right road if I went down the wrong road first. It practised what they call Tough Love ...

A NAN'S WORLD

As a medium, I don't edit myself. I just tune in and tell the story that I'm being told by spirit. The consequences of this can be dramatic, as I've discovered frequently.

One bright, summer morning a few years ago, a rather gentle middle-aged lady came to see me for a sitting. She was quite well-heeled and obviously had a bit of money, judging from the flash car she'd parked outside my studio. Almost immediately she entered the room I felt the presence of another, much older woman. She reminded me very much of my nan: like her, this lady was a very strong personality and wasted no time in speaking her mind.

She showed me an image of a man sitting at a computer, chatting with a pretty woman online. The moment I described this the woman sort of froze and closed up.

'Your nan is saying that you're living in a vicious circle. You've got to stop your husband doing what he's doing,' I said. 'And this time you've got to mean what you say.'

The lady look at me sheepishly and sort of nodded. 'Anything else?' she said.

'Well, to be honest, not a lot,' I said. 'She wants you to know that she loves you, obviously, but that is the main message she wanted to get through to you.'

The lady was clearly in need of someone to talk to, so after the sitting was over we had a cup of tea and a chat. She became much more open at this point and told me that her marriage had been in a lot of trouble. Her husband had started seeing a woman that he'd 'met' on the internet via some dating site. She'd found out about it and given him an ultimatum: stop seeing this woman or their marriage was over.

It had seemed like he had chosen the first option and she had begun working hard to breathe some life back into her marriage. But then she had grown suspicious that it had started again. Her instincts were to give her husband one final chance. But this time, she had to carry out her threat.

She'd been hoping to get a message from her nan because she had always been the woman to whom she'd turn in these situations. She wasn't so close to her mother. Her nan was the one on whom she relied to give her straightforward, no-nonsense advice. She had a saying that she used to sum up the wisdom she'd accumulated through her long life: 'It's a nan's world,' she'd say.

Sure enough, her nan had come through to her. And she'd spoken just as plainly as she'd always done in life. I had a sneaking feeling that her words were going to resolve her granddaughter's problems, one way or the other.

TRUTH TABLETS

The way in which spirits influence our lives isn't always black and white. It is subtler than that. It's much more about shades of grey. So, for instance, there have been occasions when spirits have given me warnings that I've ignored. They have then resorted to more devious measures to keep me out of trouble.

An example of this happened a few years back when I went on a date with a guy. He'd invited me out to dinner with him at a nice restaurant. I was quite looking forward to it, but as I pulled up in my car at the restaurant a voice in my head sent me a message. It was very simple and direct and was as clear as if someone was talking to me from the passenger seat. It said: 'He will hurt you. Go home.'

I'd received messages like this before in my life. When I was a teenager, walking home one evening, for instance, I'd been approached by a guy who'd pulled up alongside me in his car asking for directions. Before I could even process what he was saying to me I'd heard a voice in my head telling me to 'run'. I'd listened and raced home as fast as my legs could carry me. I later found out that the guy was a known child abductor. I was told that I'd had a very lucky escape.

So I knew the importance that these messages could carry. On this occasion, however, I chose to ignore it. I parked the car and headed into the restaurant to meet the guy.

He was a perfectly nice man, or at least he seemed to be on first impressions. He placed great store by the fact that he was a Roman Catholic and attended church quite a lot. He knew vaguely what I did for a living but didn't make any judgments about that. In fact, he barely referred to it. It didn't seem to interest him, which, to be honest, was a relief to me. It can be draining having to justify yourself twenty-four hours a day.

We had quite an enjoyable meal and left on good terms. Heading home I remembered the message I'd got but decided that perhaps it related to someone or something else. I wrote it off as a miscommunication between me and the spirit world.

A week or two later I arranged to go out with the guy a second time. Again, looking back on it now, I can see that the spirit world really didn't want me to go. The warning was even clearer. Spirit contrived in every way possible to make me late.

I was going to drive to the date but couldn't find my car keys for love nor money. When I did eventually find them I saw that I was low on petrol then discovered that the nearest petrol station had run out of fuel. I just managed to limp the car to another station nearby but had to take a detour that left me stuck in the most horrendous traffic. Inevitably, I arrived at the restaurant more than half an hour late.

A part of me wondered whether he'd given up on me and gone home. But as I pulled up outside I saw a text from him saying he was still there. I walked into the restaurant looking forward to dinner, a nice glass of wine and finding out a bit more about this guy. I didn't by any stretch of the imagination think he was future husband material. I'm not sure if that person even exists. But I did wonder whether it had the makings of a serious relationship. It didn't take long for those illusions to be well and truly shattered.

From the moment I said 'hi' the atmosphere of the evening was totally different from the first date. There was something stand-offish and a bit arrogant about him this time. He also seemed to have developed a dislike for what I did for a living. His words to me were along the lines of: 'If I was with you I would destroy that part of your life.' I don't know whether he meant he would destroy my reputation, destroy my belief in the spirit world or destroy it intellectually. I had no idea but I also had no interest in finding out what it meant.

He also kept going on about the fact that I was some kind of 'celebrity', which I really don't consider myself to be. I just do what I do. I just happen to have done it on television and at theatres quite a lot. But not everyone knows who I am, far from it. I can walk around most places unrecognised.

But he said that he wouldn't like the fact that I'd always be in the limelight, always getting attention. It was a real Dr Jekyll and Mr Hyde scenario. He was a completely different person.

We'd been together for less than fifteen minutes when I made the decision. By now I'd got the message. The warning on the first date, the trouble getting to the restaurant, and now this revelation of his true identity – it all added up to one thing. It was quite obvious that the man was 1,000 per cent wrong for me. So I made a very poor excuse about needing to get ready for a demonstration the next evening and not feeling very well and left him there. He wasn't best pleased, but I really didn't care.

As I tried to work out what had happened on the way home, I was still struggling to believe the transformation in the guy's personality from the first time we'd met. I joked with myself that it was almost as if someone had slipped him a truth drug. But then I began thinking about it and realised this was something that often happened to people around me. People just start blurting out the truth. It was then that I wondered whether it was spirit, protecting me.

It would be easy for me to ask for some kind of twenty-four-hour protection, to put out a thought that would have the spirit world on guard all the time. But I don't do that. It's actually very rare that I ask for help. I leave it to them and assume that, if it's serious, they will get involved.

As I have explained, we don't need to be protected all the time. In fact we shouldn't be – we need to make our own mistakes. We should all be like the child running down the hill sometimes. On this occasion, however, I think spirit did intervene. I'm really grateful for the fact it did.

OUT OF CONTROL

As a medium, I do have a great deal of power. And with power comes responsibility. There have been times when I've failed to live up to that responsibility, I must admit.

One moment in particular always springs to mind. It wasn't my finest hour – in fact it might have been one of my worst moments as a medium. I acted badly and irresponsibly. I still regret it to this day.

It happened one Friday evening at the end of a really busy week when I'd gone for a drink with my brother and some other friends. We'd gone to a pub in the Hertfordshire countryside that was a particular favourite of mine. I knew the landlord and they knew me. It had always been a place where I could go and have a quiet drink without people pestering me. That doesn't happen a lot, but when it does it can be annoying. Unfortunately, on that particular evening, the pub wasn't such a safe haven.

We'd had a few drinks when a group of builders came in for their Friday-night session. Among them was a guy called Nick, who had done some work on my centre. We'd become quite friendly and he'd taken a bit of an interest in what I did. However, he had been due to have a stag night at one point and I'd told him not to bother. 'The marriage will only last four months, so I wouldn't waste the money,' I had said to him. Ever since then he had carried around the idea that I'd cursed him because, sure enough, she left him after four months.

Obviously Nick had shared this story with his mates, because the minute they arrived they started glancing over at our table. After a couple of pints one of them headed to the toilet but made a point of coming past us. Without any warning he just said: 'Oh, you're the freak.' He was an ordinary-looking bloke, in his fifties, and hadn't seemed nasty. But I was thrown by this and turned my back on them.

Unfortunately, they weren't so ready to let it drop. They kept coming past me all evening, making funny faces or whispering under their breath. It all came to a head when I went up to the bar to order a drink. This guy came up to me again, clearly looking to start an argument.

'What happens if I touch you?' he said.

He was really upsetting me. I was trying to have a quiet drink at the end of a long, hard week. I really didn't need it. That didn't excuse what I did, however.

Something inside me snapped and I just said, in front of his friends: 'You've loaned someone £13,000 and you aren't going to get it back.' The bloke standing next to him went pale because basically I was talking about him. This was the signal for all of the guys to weigh in. One of them, a dark-haired guy, started waving his arms and making all sorts of accusations. He called me a fake and a cheat. He basically disrespected and tried to demolish everything that I stood for – and had worked for half my life. So, once again, my better nature failed me and I fought back.

'Your dad is standing behind you; he died four months ago and his name was Ray. And he thought you were a bit of an idiot too,' I said.

The bloke couldn't handle this. He kept saying: 'No, no, no, stop her!'

I wasn't proud of it at all. I had lost control and I really hated myself for it. My brother and I left soon after that. I had let myself down and more importantly I had let the spirit world down. I still wince at the memory of my outburst today.

Being a medium, you have power. You hold people's emotions in your hands and you should respect that. You have to be aware of people's emotions. I have avoided going to pubs and even drinking since then.

INSTANT KARMA

Some people are under the impression that mediums and psychics get preferential treatment from the spirit world. They seem to imagine that, because we are more closely attuned to the Other Side, we somehow get a kind of VIP, red carpet service. That's really not the case, I can assure you.

It's really important that we also experience all the emotions – good and bad – that everyone else experiences, for a couple of reasons. Firstly, it helps us to be more sympathetic and understanding as mediums. How are we going to offer advice and guidance to someone going through bereavement or illness or a personal crisis if we haven't experienced those things ourselves?

But secondly it's also important for the development of our soul. As I've explained, this life is where our soul learns the great lessons each of us needs to experience at some stage of our ongoing existence. So we need to feel the wounds before we go on to the spirit world where our soul heals.

Having said this, however, I have encountered a couple of instances where those in the spirit world have extended a friendly hand to those who have served it particularly well. One occasion that really sticks in my mind concerned a lady who came for a sitting with me a few years back. Her name was Jay and she was a truly beautiful soul.

She'd been raised in the Spiritualist movement and was

very close to one of its great twentieth-century figures, Gordon Higginson. Gordon is regarded by most people as the outstanding British medium of the last hundred years and was head of the Spiritualists National Union and principal at the Arthur Findlay College in Stansted, Essex where I did some of my development work. He had been very close to Jay's mother, who was also a healer and a medium. Gordon had been a grandfather figure to Jay when she was growing up. When he died in 1993 she'd felt his loss deeply.

The moment I began sitting for Jay, I felt a very powerful wave of energy. It was as if a large number of spirits were trying to come through to me at once, almost in a collective voice. And they were trying to pass on one word to me: karma.

I truly believe that the spirit world operates on the basis of karma. In other words, you get back what you have put in. In a way, I suppose, this does equate to the religious notion of those who have done good work on this earth being rewarded in heaven. I don't think of it that way, of course. But I do believe it's a powerful principle nevertheless.

In this case, it soon became clear to me that this related directly to Jay and her family. I began to sense that her mother, who was still in this world, was unwell. Jay nodded at me when I said this. So I simply passed on the message as I had been presented it.

'Don't worry, your mum is going to be OK,' I told her. 'Karma is going to make sure of that.'

Afterwards, she told me that her mother was desperately ill with a mysterious condition that doctors were struggling to diagnose. 'We really don't know if she is going to make it,' she told me.

There was a quiet strength and dignity about her, which was, I'm sure, a lot to do with her Spiritualist faith. Even if the worst did come to pass, I knew she could sleep safe in the knowledge that there was another life on the Other Side of this one. She knew that the spirit world was there waiting to welcome her mother and reunite her with those to whom she was closest.

I stayed in contact with Jay afterwards. I liked her but I was also keen to hear about her mother's progress. I was, to be honest, intrigued by what this message had meant exactly.

Jay was kind enough to drop me a note or give me a quick call every now and again over the coming months. The news she passed on was verging on the miraculous. Despite the worst prognoses of some of the doctors, Jay's mother came through the immediate crisis. That was surprising enough. But she then began to turn a corner and make a full recovery, something the doctors hadn't thought possible. A year on her near miraculous recovery was complete and she was living a full and fulfilling life.

There was no question in my mind that the spirit world had played a huge role in this. As I'd sensed myself, there was a huge well of energy taking an interest in Jay's mother. And a lot of that energy was a karmic reaction to all the positive energy that Jay's mother had put out into this world – and the next one – through her work as a medium and a healer. All the goodness she'd put out was coming back at her. It was almost as if spirit had decided to thank her for what she had done and given her the gift of an extended life.

It was one of the most beautiful things I've encountered in my time as a medium.

FATHER'S DAY

Being a medium is never easy. You can't remain immune from the realities of life – and death. Both are just as much a part of your world as they are for everyone else. I suppose if there is a difference it is that, if we are lucky, we will use the negative experiences in our lives in a positive way. No one has exemplified this better than a young student whom I taught a few years back, Chris. He was a very bright, warm-hearted young man who joined a six-month course I was running introducing people to the art of mediumship.

I spotted that Chris was a smart individual early on. I could see that he had potential. He seemed to have a natural ability to tune into spirit. All he needed was to learn how to interpret and communicate to others the messages that he received. In that respect, he was no different from any other young medium. I'd been in the same position myself a couple of decades ago.

I was watching Chris's development with real interest, but then, just a few weeks into the course, something happened that threatened to disrupt his development. We were working on the principles of Tarot reading. I invited Chris to pick a card and he turned over an image of an angelic woman walking up some stairs. Tarot is like other aspects of the psychic and mediumistic art – it is open to interpretation. So he could have taken this card in a number of ways. But for some reason he just looked at me and said: 'Tracy, I think this card is showing me that my dad is going to die.'

I was slightly taken aback. I wasn't sure how I would have interpreted that card. It wasn't a death card, so it did leave open quite a few possibilities. He'd taken it as a 'Stairway to Heaven' image. That could have been right. But equally it could have been wrong. I wasn't sure. Before I could really respond, however, Chris looked at me and asked me straight. 'What should I do about it?' he said.

When you are a medium you are given extremely sensitive and powerful information on a regular basis and have to be very careful about how you handle that information. Teaching other mediums how to deal with this very tricky area is one of the hardest things I have to do. It's always a tough call. But I knew I had to give him an honest answer.

I didn't validate what he'd said. I didn't tell him that his dad was going to pass, not least because I knew that he was very close to him. So I just told him to make sure he spent some decent time with his father in the weeks and months ahead.

But I didn't do this knowing anything, one way or the other. What I said to him was a variation on what I say to a lot of people: 'We are all going to go one day, so make the most of every day in this life. It might well be that you do that for the next twenty years. But at least you've acted.'

As it transpired, however, Chris and his dad didn't have that long. As the course continued, Chris let us know that his father had, indeed, become terminally ill. He had been given a matter of weeks to live. Chris's reading had been 100 per cent correct. His father passed during the last month of the six-month course.

On the last weekend of the course, the students had to demonstrate to the public and the rest of the class. It was a charity event. Chris was an absolute beginner and he'd missed one of the sessions because his dad had passed. But he turned up on that final day smartly dressed in a suit, which I'm sure his dad would have been very proud about, ready to demonstrate. Some students don't take it seriously. He came through dressed like a professional medium even though he was a beginner.

During the course of his fifteen-minute demonstration that day he brought through two different fathers and handled it with the most amazing composure. I'm not sure I would have been able to handle it myself. I remember being in tears on stage when I connected to a mother the day after the funeral of my great friend and mentor Hilary Goldman. Yet Chris didn't crack even though his dad had been gone only two weeks.

Chris has since headed around the world travelling, and is now holding sittings in Australia. He is still a young man and has a long time to develop and progress as a medium. Given the dignity and professionalism Chris displayed that day, I have no doubt that, one day, he will be a truly great medium. I hope I am around – in this life or the next one – to witness it.

Spirit Truth: spirit will show you what's necessary to bring people comfort

---

The power of the Afterlife is remarkable. It can make me do – and say – things that I wouldn't dream of doing or saying ordinarily. Often I will use phrases or words that I would never ever dream of using. For instance, I remember one night getting a terrible stinging pain in my leg. I described it as being exactly like a wasp bite and it turned out that the spirit I was connecting with had died of a wasp bite. However, I have no idea what a wasp bite feels like. I've never had one – and have no intention of getting one if I can help it!

Another strong example of this kind of experience happened one night recently, when I was demonstrating at a theatre in Shrewsbury. Midway through the evening, I was joined by the spirit of a man in overalls. He walked on stage and put a workman's bag down. I could see that it was a plumber's toolkit.

'I don't know if we've got a problem with the plumbing here in the theatre but I've just been joined by a plumber,' I said, to roars of laughter from the audience.

His name was Tony and he was very keen to communicate with me; he kept going on about two characters, Big John and Little John. For a moment I wondered if it was something to do with Robin Hood, but the message was moving towards a lady in the front row. It turned out that this lady's husband was called Big John and her son was Little John. But it didn't feel like Tony was a family connection. It actually felt like he was a plumber.

Tony kept showing me all sorts of images, one of which was something that was marked Saniflo. I was also shown a red handle, the sort of thing that you'd see on pipe-work in your boiler room. It was as if the plumbing had been put in back to front. The lady was roaring with laughter. It turned out that Tony was a friend of her husband's, a real plumber who had passed recently. He had been watching her having central heating put into her house and it had all been done badly. The red thing hadn't been put in properly and this had affected the Saniflo, whatever that was. The upshot of all this was that the whole job would have to be done again. It had been completely botched up.

There I was, using all this technical jargon. I had no idea what I was saying but I was talking as if I was a City & Guilds qualified plumber.

If there is a USP, a unique selling point, to what I do, it is that I get this kind of detail from spirit. It's what I believe all mediums should be doing. Far too many of them are content to tell people, 'I've got your gran here and she's got grey hair'. Well, whoop-diddly-doo! That's not evidence. Everyone's gran has got grey hair pretty much.

One of my students, Dave, asked me, 'How do you get the information you get, because you don't get the normal stuff?'

My answer to him was simple: 'Because I don't expect the normal stuff.'

When I'm sitting for someone, I imagine that I'm the person who is receiving the message. And I know that person wants to know that their mum, dad, wife, husband, son, daughter or whoever is all right. So I don't want to know what colour their hair is or how tall they are. Who cares? If you are in spirit, why would you bother to come back to talk about that? Wouldn't you come back to say something interesting? So it does surprise, but that's what I want, because I want it to be 100 per cent right.

I'm quite hard on myself for that reason.

A very well-regarded medium, Eileen Davies, once told me that she felt sorry for my guides. 'Your poor guides, the things you put them through,' she said to me. But my view is that it's my role to give evidence that life continues. And for that evidence to be credible it has to be different.

**Spirit Truth: mediums don't have a 'direct line'
to the spirit world**

THE BLUE SHIRT

There's a widespread assumption that if you are a medium you can connect with the Other Side at will. People imagine it's as if we are constantly plugged in. All we need to do is tune in and have a conversation with anyone we want in the spirit world. It's like picking up the telephone or switching on a light. The truth is, however, it's nothing like that.

Again, the easiest way to explain it is to draw a parallel with the real world. Is it that easy to talk to anyone you want whenever you want to in this existence? Of course not. You may have someone's telephone number but they aren't necessarily going to answer when you ring. They may not be at home, or it may be inconvenient. They may not want to talk to you.

If this was the case, I'd be speaking to my nan on a daily basis. She was one of the most important people in my life and I miss her physical presence all the time. I'd love to be able to talk to her whenever I'm feeling low or uncertain about something, but I can't. I've had a handful of communications with her since she passed, some of them through other mediums. That's often how it works, to be honest. A lot of mediums receive messages from their own loved ones via other mediums.

That happened to me recently when I met and began working with another medium who has since become a good friend of mine, Paul Francis. Paul is a really talented medium and a lovely person. The first time we worked together was memorable for all sorts of reasons.

Paul had been intrigued to meet me and was, he later told me, impressed by my honesty when he introduced himself as the act before mine at a demonstration we were both booked for. 'Don't be rubbish,' I apparently said to him. Paul had been performing in an earlier session which I didn't see. He then returned to the auditorium for my demonstration later in the day. It turned out he'd been very keen to see me.

Early on in the demonstration, I felt myself in the presence of a lady called Maureen, whom everyone called Mary. I felt very strongly that it was for Paul, which worried me a bit. I didn't want people to think he was some kind of plant. He obviously knew this and waited for a while before raising his hand rather sheepishly.

I made a joke of it at first. 'Are you sure it's you?' I said. 'Haven't you had enough talking to spirit today?'

I realised that I'd have to come up with something very strong to reassure the audience that this wasn't a set-up, so I started bombarding him with detail. 'If this woman is really your mother then who is Babs and who is Anne?' I asked.

At that both he and the two women sitting with him burst into laughter. 'This is Babs, my PA, and Anne, who also works with me,' he told me.

'Ah, OK,' I said.

As I connected with Mary more and more I began to sense that she really was Paul's mother. She was there to pass on a very important message, I realised.

'Sometimes we don't have confidence in ourselves. We ask ourselves whether we should be doing the job we are doing,' I told Paul. 'Your mum is telling you that you should definitely carry on. She's very proud of you.'

Paul had also recovered from cancer after a two-year battle. 'Your mum says that this is your purpose in life, this is why you are here,' I said.

At this Paul got quite emotional, so I decided to lighten things up a little. She called him a 'demented hamster' – something that, apparently, she'd done often when she was alive. But the moment that got him – and the rest of the audience – rolling in the aisles was when his mother said, through me, 'They were right, you know – you should have worn the blue shirt tonight!'

I continued, 'She says it makes your eyes shine and makes you look better. She is showing me that it's hanging in your wardrobe and asking why aren't you wearing it?'

Babs and Anne were laughing hysterically. Apparently the three of them had had an animated conversation earlier in the day about what Paul should wear on stage tonight. And he'd chosen to wear a black shirt rather than the blue one.

We all had a laugh afterwards. Paul was delighted with the message and said that it would give him the confidence to carry on after suffering a real crisis of confidence about his mediumship.

He admitted that he had been very close to quitting altogether.

But it was when he revealed something else that I realised the true significance of this message. Earlier in the day Paul had done a section in his show in which he allowed members of the audience to ask him questions. A hand had gone up in the crowd and someone asked him whether he often heard from his own family. Apparently he revealed that his mum had passed eight years earlier and he hadn't received a message from her, even through another medium.

I had no idea about this but was overwhelmed – and overjoyed – that I'd been able to bring that eight-year wait to an end.

It reminded me of how patient we have to be as mediums – and as people in general – when it comes to the spirit world. They will find us in their own good time.

Spirit Truth: **mediums aren't in constant contact with spirit**

A lot of people seem to imagine that mediums are constantly talking to the spirit world. The fact of the matter is that, unless we are working, of course, we are rarely in touch with the Other Side.

Why? Well, the main difference between mediums and other people is that mediums know the spirit world is there. We don't need to see any proof or evidence. We just know it. So we don't have spirits hanging around us 24/7. Again, the comparison is with real life. I wouldn't have my nan or my granddad or my friends who have passed over hanging around me 24/7 in this life. So why would they be doing it now that they in the spirit world? It makes no sense. If my nan was still alive, I would know that she would be living in her house on the same street and that if I needed her I would pop round to see her or pick up the phone and call her. She'd be there if I needed her.

When I started working, my granddad Stanley was my first real spirit helper. He was there all the time. But again, I've not relied on him so much in recent years. There are times when he comes to my aid. Recently, for instance, I was feeling a little low, and needed a little boost. All of a sudden I kept seeing Stanley Street, wherever I went. That always gives me a gee-up. I saw the road name in Devon, in North Wales, south Wales, Swindon. And that's all I needed – I knew he was there.

So, as I say, I very rarely ask spirit for anything for myself. I don't need them – and, more to the point, they don't need us. It must be very annoying for spirits to have to prove themselves all the time. So many people seem to want them to materialise in front of them and say 'boo'. Having said all that, of course, there are times when we need help, a little more solid guidance in life.

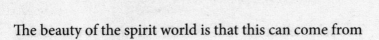
The beauty of the spirit world is that this can come from an infinite number of sources.

I've been fortunate to have a few such spirits in my life.

THE SEQUINED DRESS

In the summer of 2011 I was very busy both at work and in my private life. I was in the process of moving to a new home as well as running classes and touring the UK and Ireland extensively. So there were times when I barely had a moment to myself. Throughout this period, however, I was being told that I needed to take care of a good friend of mine, and more specifically her mother.

I've written about my friend Mariolanda before. She is one of the closest and most loyal friends I have. Her mother, Nina, was dear to me as well. She was from a very feisty, Sicilian family and was someone who told it exactly like it was.

On more than one occasion when I had been feeling sorry for myself, Nina had given me a stern talking-to. Once, when I'd been on the verge of giving up my mediumship altogether she'd told me: 'Tracy, just get off your backside and get back to work; you've got a job to do, so do it and shut up with your complaining.' I really liked her for that. She'd been more of a help to me than she'd realised.

So when the spirits began to show me images of her being unwell, I knew I had to be there for her. Mariolanda was pregnant at the time as well, so I knew it was doubly important that I help them both. Despite my hectic schedule, I rang Mariolanda a couple of times to warn her about what I'd been sensing.

'You really need to get Nina to a doctor,' I said.

She said she'd talk to her mother but didn't hold out much hope of her paying much attention. 'You know what she's like,' she said.

Sure enough, when Mariolanda passed on my concerns, Nina dismissed them with a flamboyant wave of her hand. She was adamant that she was fine and wasn't going to see any doctors. Ordinarily I'd have admired her strength of character. This time, however, I knew that she was being too stubborn for her own good.

Eventually, matters were taken out of Nina's hands. Late that summer she began having dizzy spells. During a brief conversation one night, Mariolanda told me that her mum was falling over frequently and had been referred to a specialist. Nina was admitted to hospital where they found she had a tumour in her brain.

Everyone was deeply worried about the operation, which was risky in the extreme. The doctors had warned that there was a danger Nina could suffer minor brain damage if the op didn't go precisely according to plan. So everyone breathed a huge sigh of relief when everything went well in the operating theatre.

But it turned out that we'd been premature in assuming Nina was out of the woods. Around forty-eight hours after the op, as she was seemingly recovering in hospital, she complained of feeling dizzy again. Before the medics could get to her, she had collapsed in her husband's arms and passed away.

I got the news on the day that I was physically moving house. I wasn't entirely surprised when the phone call came via a friend that evening. As I'd spent the day carting packing cases in and out of a removal truck, I'd been getting more and more messages about Nina. I'd also been shown an image that I didn't yet understand but which clearly related to her and Mariolanda. It was of a big emerald ring.

I was really upset by Nina's passing, even though I knew she was beginning a new existence in spirit. I was going to miss her personality and sheer lust for life. I spoke to Mariolanda several times in the days that followed. She asked me to let her know if I received any messages from her mother. I was able to pass on a couple of small, simple messages but it was at her funeral that I got the most dramatic intimation of Nina's new existence in spirit. It was a moment that I will never forget as long as I remain in this life.

Going to a funeral is not a great experience for a medium, especially when it involves someone you have known very well and loved. When you are sensitive as we are, it can be overwhelming.

The service was being held at a big Catholic church in Hoddesdon. I was in a very fragile state when I arrived so I sat at the back in the last row at the very edge. I thought if I couldn't handle it and I got overwhelmed by all the energy in there I would slip out without Mariolanda and her family knowing. I didn't want to make a scene.

The service was a huge affair. It was absolutely rammed inside the church with people standing along the side of the pews and even a small crowd gathered outside, listening in. As the service got under way I focused on Mariolanda and her brothers. I could see the aura around them. There was a lot of energy and there were lights coming and going. I sensed the presence of spirit, although not Nina herself at that point.

The service was an elaborate one, partly in Italian. As the priest spoke in Nina's native tongue, I confess I drifted off briefly. I had a million thoughts flying around in my mind. But then, for some reason, I looked back towards the tabernacle section of the church, where I saw the priest heading in readiness for giving out Holy Communion. Along with some altar boys, he was taking the golden goblet and the plates for the Communion bread from the place where they were kept between services. It was then that I saw Nina.

I once read a book called *The Shack*, about a father who is grieving the murder of his daughter, and who is invited, seemingly by God, to the deserted shack where the killing happened. Without giving too much away, the central character, Mack, sees a vision of the Holy Spirit which is described as shimmering in light.

This is exactly the form in which I now saw Nina. She was hovering above the tabernacle, shimmering as if the sun was hitting her and reflected in a million tiny beams of golden light. As if to make her glow even more brightly, she was wearing an amazing, glittering dress made of sequins. She looked absolutely fabulous, slim and healthy.

I tried my best to disguise the shock that I was feeling. It was clear that Nina was trying to speak to me, however. I kept hearing a voice saying: 'You can hear me, can't you, Tracy?' It was as clear as if she was sitting next to me.

I was too fragile to deal with it at that point. I also knew that it would probably freak out most of the congregation if I told anyone what I could see. So, as gently and kindly as I could, I sent a thought to Nina. 'Not today, Nina, please not today.'

In life she hadn't been a woman to take no for an answer, and she wasn't any different now that she'd passed into spirit. 'As long as you remember everything and tell Mariolanda about it the next time you see her,' she told me.

A couple of things struck me about her. Firstly, she remained exactly the same fiery, no-nonsense figure in the spirit world. I smiled inwardly at the thought of her locking horns with other spirits.

The other thing that struck me was how amazing she looked. Nina had struggled with her weight throughout her life. She was always on diets. As I looked at her shimmering above the congregation I could see that her skin looked great. She was wearing make-up and looked a million dollars in her sequined dress.

She had probably been in view for about a minute when she began to fade. She left with one final reminder. 'Don't forget. Tell her everything.'

Two weeks later I got a text from Mariolanda saying she was off to the hospital for a scan that morning and wanted to pop in for a cup of tea on the way home. I knew exactly what she had in mind. She wanted to grill me on whether I'd seen or heard anything from her mother. 'Come on then, tell me,' she said. 'I know you saw something.'

I remembered what her mother had told me in church, so recounted every detail. At first, as I described the shimmering apparition I'd seen, Mariolanda looked at me as if I was mad. But her expression changed when I described the sequined dress and how great her mother looked in it.

'She'd worn that dress to my wedding. You weren't there so you never saw it. She'd slimmed down for the wedding and had lost weight again in the last few weeks of her life and had been talking about wearing it again. So my dad and I put her in it. We were the only ones who saw her in the coffin,' she told me, dabbing away a tear.

Mariolanda gave birth to a baby boy, Frankie, a few months later. I went round to her house to see her and give her a present for the baby.

As we spoke, I noticed Mariolanda was wearing a ring, an emerald ring, just like the one I'd seen on the day of Nina's passing. I asked her about it.

'It was Mum's,' she told me. 'It was one of her favourites. She left it to me and I wore it to the funeral. To be honest I only wear it now and again. Why d'you ask?'

'I'd look after it, if I was you. I've got a feeling that it might be the best way for you to stay close to your mum,' I said, smiling.

I've felt Nina's spirit around me several times since then. She's the same, straight-talking, no-holds-barred personality that she always was. A couple of times I've been feeling low about something and I've heard her say simply, 'Stop it, pull yourself together.' She's the sort of spirit I need every now and again, to be honest. I hope she remains around me – and Mariolanda – for many years to come.

PART FOUR:
The Truth about Messages from the Other Side

'Do for this life as if you live forever,
do for the Afterlife as if you die tomorrow.'
Ali ibn Abi Talib

Another of the great misapprehensions people have about mediumship and the spirit world is that the messages we receive from the Other Side come in a familiar form. They don't. As a medium, I receive messages in all sorts of forms, from direct conversations with spirits to subtle signs that take the form of thoughts, images, pieces of music and even smells. In this section I will share some of the truths I have learned about messages from the Other Side.

GOLDEN THREADS

People expect the spirits of their loved ones to talk to them in the same way that they did when they were in this world. Why?

Messages can take all sorts of forms. During the course of my career, I have relayed thousands of communications. Many have been complex and lengthy. But others have been very simple and direct. In some instances, they have been signs rather than direct communications. But often these very simple messages have also been the most profound.

Many times, these have been small signs or a simple comment that has provided the proof that families desperately need sometimes of their loved ones' ongoing existence. I call these kind of messages 'golden threads', because they offer a priceless link between the two worlds. A few stick in my memory more clearly than others.

The first came when I was demonstrating in Llandudno in North Wales. My family on my father's side have Welsh roots, so I always feel at home there. This particular evening's demonstration had been a good one, alive with really strong connections and messages. Afterwards, as usual, I sat and signed copies of my books for members of the audience.

Often, this is an opportunity for people who haven't received a message during the demonstration to say hello to me. And they sometimes come in the hope that they can receive a message now. This is rarely possible because I'm disconnected from the spirit world at this point; I'm more focused on spelling people's names correctly when I sign their books!

Occasionally, however, I do make a connection. That's what happened on this evening.

A mother and daughter were standing in the queue, waiting patiently to see me. I noticed them when they were about three or four places from the front of the line and I could tell that they were both very emotional. The mother was shaking like a leaf.

They wanted to buy one of my books but by the time they got to the head of the queue there were none left. I think everyone in the queue could sense how much in pain this couple were, so rather wonderfully, the lady in front of them offered the mother the copy she'd just bought. The mother and her daughter were so grateful.

When they got to me, they asked me to make the dedication in their book to Ann and Margaret. As we chatted the daughter asked me whether it would be possible for her mother to have a one-to-one session with me. The mother had barely been able to speak a word as she stood there. Her shaking was, if anything, more pronounced than it had been earlier. I could tell she wasn't ready for a one-to-one with me. She was still going through the grieving process.

But I was able to offer her some solace.

As we spoke the mother placed in front of me a

photograph of her son. He was a handsome-looking young lad in a white T-shirt. I wasn't sure what to do at first, but fortunately the spirit world soon took over. I began to see images of red – red scarves, red shirts. They were all connected to Manchester United. I then saw a figure standing behind the two ladies. It was a young boy, and he was wearing the famous red and white kit.

The instant I explained this to the two ladies, their reaction was dramatic. The mother was so overwhelmed she nearly fell over. A couple of people in the queue behind her had to hold on to her for a second. She'd soon recovered her composure, however.

'Obviously you understand this,' I said to them.

'Yes, yes, that's right,' the daughter said. 'That's Sean. My brother. He died two weeks ago.'

They explained to me that Sean had been a passionate Man United fan. He watched every match on television and regularly travelled to Manchester to see his idols. So when he was buried he was given a Manchester United-themed funeral. He was dressed in a Man United shirt, there were photos of his favourite players with him and the casket was threaded with Man United scarves.

I told the ladies that I would be willing to do a fuller reading with them when they were feeling stronger. But I could see as they left that what they'd received already was a huge relief and comfort for them.

Sometimes, all people need is to know that their loved ones are safe and are continuing their existence on the Other Side. All they need is the tiniest sliver of information. These golden threads keep them tethered and connected to their loved ones.

THE FINAL HANDSHAKE

A golden thread can be the tiniest thing. It can seem almost inconsequential to those who aren't receiving the message. But to those that do get a communication, it can be truly wonderful, as if a light has suddenly been switched on in their life.

I've been lucky enough to have passed on many such messages over the years. One that always sticks in my mind happened one night when I was demonstrating in Sheffield. Midway through the evening, I got a message from a lady in spirit. Her name was Sylvia and she had passed quite recently at a very advanced age. She was trying to connect with her daughter and granddaughter, who she was telling me were both in the audience.

As I say, the information I receive from spirit can comes in all forms – from the spoken word to feelings and sounds to images. Sylvia was connecting to me in quite an unusual way in that she was showing me a lot of images, some of which made sense and some of which did not. Fortunately, I was able to interpret and pass on enough information to connect the lady with a mother and daughter who were sitting towards the front of the theatre. They were delighted to hear from Sylvia. As the message continued, however, there was one particular image that kept imposing itself on my mind that I simply couldn't put it into words.

I decided there was only one option. 'Could you come and speak to me after the show?' I said. 'There's something I need to tell you but I can't speak it, I will have to show it to you.'

I'm sure the two ladies felt a mixture of intrigue and apprehension as they sat through the rest of the show wondering what on earth I had in store.

As I arrived in the foyer of the theatre at the end of the evening, I saw that the pair were towards the front of the long queue that almost always forms as people wait to get a signed book or autograph. They introduced themselves as Mary and Melanie. When I extended my hand to shake Mary – the mother's – hand, I could see clearly the image that her mother had shown me on stage.

So I adjusted my hand and held her hand in a very specific way. It was almost like a Freemason's handshake. I clasped her hand with my thumb rubbing over the space between her thumb and first finger.

She looked at me a little uncertainly at first. 'That's where you were holding your mother's hand when she passed,' I said. 'That's what she was showing me when I was on stage.'

Mary's reaction was wonderful. Her face lit up like a child's on Christmas morning. 'Oh that's wonderful,' she said. 'Absolutely wonderful. Everything else you gave us in the theatre was lovely. Absolutely perfect. But to know that she showed you that last, precious moment we shared together, a moment that nobody else in this world knew about, means everything to me.'

It reminded me of how subtle yet powerful mediumship can be. It also reminded me of the fact that messages don't need to be spectacular or sensational to make an impact on people's hearts.

Sometimes it is the thinnest of golden threads that offer the strongest and most secure links to the Other Side.

SCRATCHES ON THE LINO

I was demonstrating in Basildon, in Essex, one evening when I got a message from a dad who was trying to connect with his daughter. I was soon drawn towards a young woman sitting towards the rear of the theatre. She was a little reluctant to accept that the man was her father, however. I quickly realised that I'd need to give her some very detailed information in order to validate this message.

This, of course, is my job. I understand entirely that people, even those who believe in my work and the existence of the Afterlife, need to be certain that I am connecting them with the spirit of their loved one. I need to offer proof rather than evidence.

I told the young lady that her father's name was Norman and that, judging from the tightness I was experiencing in my chest, he had died of heart and lung problems.

She nodded at all this, but seemed underwhelmed, to be honest. I think she thought I was simply making lucky guesses. All that changed, however, when I made what seemed to me an off-hand comment.

At first I wasn't even sure I should say it. 'He's saying, "Don't stress about the scratches on the lino", I said, almost apologetically, not sure it was worth saying.

But the minute the words left my mouth, the young lady nearly fell off her chair. 'That's it,' she said, punching the air. 'That's all I needed, that must be my dad. That's exactly the sort of thing he'd say.'

After the show she told me that she'd had new furniture in her home but the delivery men had somehow scratched the linoleum in her hallway as they carried it into the house. She'd been stressing about it, but that message from her dad had put everything in perspective for her. His seemingly flippant little remark about the lino meant more to her than the fact that I'd named him and told her what he'd passed from.

It was another example of the power of simplicity in mediumship. They say that God is in the detail and that is so true, regardless of what you think God might be. They can seem like tiny little things but these simple messages can have immense meaning for people.

JACKY'S VOICE

We are all capable of receiving messages from the spirit world. And many of us do receive them – day in day out. Unfortunately, not everyone is able or willing to pay heed to these messages.

Someone who did listen, however, was a lady called Jacky.

She came to my centre for a one-to-one sitting. She seemed a very chilled-out and relaxed lady and was very comfortable in the room. I sensed she had received communications from spirit before and would be someone who attracted energy very easily. And so it proved.

I'd soon connected to the spirit of an elderly lady who began to show me a series of images of Jacky in hospital. I saw her in what looked like one of those cat-scan machines and her head being X-rayed. I then saw her being wheeled into an operating theatre.

'I am seeing you going in for a major operation. I am feeling a pain in my head. Does that mean anything to you?' I said to her.

She just nodded as if to say 'go on'.

As I continued to tune into this energy, I saw Jacky lying in bed with bandages on her head, but smiling and chatting happily to visitors.

'Spirit are telling me that they are glad you heeded their warning,' I said.

She smiled at this. 'I'd like to thank them for giving me that warning,' she replied.

Afterwards, over a cup of tea, she told me what had happened. She'd been a pretty fit and healthy individual until one day she started getting really terrible headaches. She took painkillers and got her eyes tested. She did all the usual things, in other words, but the pains not only persisted – they got worse.

As they did so, she began to have dizzy spells and lose her balance. She also felt lethargic and lacking in energy. She was on a downward spiral. Sometimes she'd felt like she was having a stroke, she told me. At other times, she had such blinding headaches that she almost felt as if she was having visions. She knew that she should go to see her doctor but kept putting it off in the hope that the problem would somehow disappear. It didn't.

It all came to a head one morning when Jacky got up. As she was putting on her dressing gown and getting ready to go downstairs for a morning cup of tea, she heard a voice talking to her. It was as clear as if it had come from a person standing right next to her. It said: 'You have a brain tumour; you are going to have radiotherapy but you are going to be OK.'

Now, a lot of people would have dismissed this as a symptom of her illness. They would have written it off as paranoia brought on by the tiredness she'd been experiencing. But Jacky was different. She was a firm believer in mediumship and the spirit world. She also shared my own very strong conviction that spirit is communicating with all of us all the time. They are offering us guidance and advice on a 24/7 basis. We just need to tune into it sometimes.

Jacky recognised this message as an intervention by spirit and realised that she had to take it seriously and act immediately. So that's exactly what she did. That morning she made an appointment to see her doctor. He recognised the symptoms and referred her straightaway for a brain scan at her nearest hospital. They discovered a brain tumour the size of a large grape or a fig. Within a very short period of time, only a few weeks I think, Jacky was beginning a course of radiotherapy.

It wasn't pleasant, of course. She suffered a lot of the normal side effects, from tiredness and feeling sick, to vomiting and a little bit of hair loss. But she came through it. By the end of the first course of therapy, the tumour had shrunk to the size of a blueberry, and was getting smaller all the time. The doctors' prognosis was positive. Jacky looked like she was going to come through.

People often ask me whether they can ask the spirit world for help in dealing with the problems that life throws at them. My answer is no – and yes. The spirit world is not able to prevent you going through emotional crises, whether it's the end of a relationship or mourning the loss of a loved one. Your soul has to experience an element of pain in this life so that it can learn and grow. It will then heal in the next life.

Having said this, however, spirit can offer you guidance if you ask for it. But you have to be attuned, you have to be ready to hear it, as Jacky had been. In her case, it almost certainly prolonged her life.

THE BUTTERFLY

I am constantly surprised by the way that the spirit world can manipulate people so that they end up in the right place at the right time. On countless occasions over the years, I have connected a spirit with a person who, often for reasons they can't really explain, has happened to be sitting in the church or theatre where I have been giving a demonstration.

One recent experience sticks in my mind. I was demonstrating in Blackheath Halls, a rather grand venue in south-east London. It's mainly a venue for classical music and other arty events, but there's an old recital room there which has a great atmosphere. I'd given demonstrations there a few times and always drawn a warm and responsive audience.

Early on during the demonstration I got the very strong sense of a middle-aged lady coming through to me. I sensed a familiar pain as her energy grew and saw that she had passed quite recently of cancer. She was letting me know that she wanted to connect with her sister. That was all very well, of course, but I could sense a really big problem here because there was no question in my mind that this lady – and her sister – were American and lived in the United States. I explained this to the audience and they laughed heartily. Until, that is, a lady towards the front of the room raised her hand.

'Oh, do you recognise this lady?' I said.

'Yes, I do,' she said, in an unmistakably American accent.

I was gobsmacked. 'OK, your sister had been telling me that you lived in America, but that doesn't seem to be the case,' I smiled.

'Well, I do live in America. I just happen to be here in London on business for a day or two,' she replied.

I didn't dwell on this for too long because I could sense that the spirit of her sister was anxious to connect with her. She wasn't communicating with me via words. Instead she was showing me images. The most recurrent one was of butterflies. She was basically trying to tell me that this was her favourite creature. I got the sense that she had owned a lot of jewellery and artwork depicting butterflies. I understood this, of course. I'm the same, only in my case my symbol is the dragonfly.

It was then that something extraordinary happened. As I was talking, I could feel my hand closing. I then felt a very light, tickling sensation, as if something was flapping inside my hand.

'It's as if I'm holding a butterfly,' I told the lady. I put out my hand and opened it, half expecting something to fly out. Of course, nothing did. But at that precise moment the lady stood up and stretched out her hand. When she opened it she had a butterfly-shaped brooch in her hand.

As it happened my agent, Tony, was in the audience that night. When we first started working together, he could be a bit sceptical about my work. But at the sight of this brooch he let out the loudest noise I think I'd ever heard him make. It was so noticeable other people turned round to look at him.

After the demonstration ended I couldn't resist having a chat with the American lady down in the bar area of the Halls. She was charming. She told me she was from Chicago and was travelling around Europe on business. She had a meeting in London the following day and had booked into the nearest local hotel only a few hours before the demonstration. She'd headed out that evening not quite sure what to do with herself. But then she'd seen a poster advertising my appearance at the Blackheath Halls and bought a ticket. Back at the hotel, she'd remembered that she always carried one of her sister's brooches with her and decided to bring it along.

There is absolutely no doubt in my mind that she was manipulated by spirit that night. They knew that her sister was ready to make a connection with me and that she needed to be in that audience. So they made it happen.

Spirit Truth: **spirit is more likely to connect in an energetic atmosphere**

I am an unconventional medium. A lot of what I do and say flies in the face of the traditions that have surrounded mediums for more than a century in this country. This isn't because I don't value or appreciate the work that traditional mediums do – quite the opposite: I wouldn't be where I am today without the help of amazingly gifted and generous mediums from the Spiritualist movement and elsewhere.

However, there are some basic principles that I fundamentally disagree with. One of them is the need to meditate. According to traditional mediumship, you need to meditate before you can make a connection with spirit. The argument is that you need to be at peace so that you can tune into the same frequency as spirit.

Often when I arrive at a church or a theatre, the organisers of events are surprised at my reaction when they ask me where I'd like to meditate before my performance. I tell them I don't need to. A lot of people don't believe me. When I arrive at a theatre at 7.25 pm for a performance that's going to start at 7.30 pm, they ask me if I'd like the opening of the demonstration postponed for fifteen minutes while I get into some transcendental state. They look shocked when I say that I'm fine and only need a couple of minutes to go to the loo and apply some lipstick.

The truth of the matter is that I can't think of anything less conducive to connecting with spirit than meditation. Why? Well, in my opinion, it is more likely to repel rather than attract spirit. I will explain why.

To understand this, you need to appreciate that we resonate at three main levels. The first is normal level, where most of us are most of the time. Second, there is a lower, relaxed level where you are at when you meditate, when all your energy is closed in on itself. And finally there's heightened energy, when we are literally 'high'. Now, this doesn't require drink or drugs – we can all get high naturally. This is the frequency at which spirit operates. So as a result, I believe you need to raise your vibration if you want to be in contact with spirit. Meditating is the last thing you need to do. If you meditate you are taking yourself twice as far away.

A few of my students disagreed with me on this. So I did an experiment recently where I tried working with my students in two different atmospheres. In the first, I let them meditate in silence before attempting to connect with spirit. In the second, I created a really high, electric energy by playing loud drumming music. The difference was striking. The messages we received in the second, more dynamic atmosphere were much more accurate and consistent and contained. The energy was also sustained for longer. It confirmed what I have long thought about meditation.

Now, this isn't to say that meditation is bad for you. It can be fabulous. Meditation is very good for the soul, for calming and spiritual peace. But I don't think you need to do that before you make a connection with spirit. As far as I'm concerned, you are cocooning yourself, you are shutting your energy down.

This is why when I am heading to a demonstration, I am working my energy levels up rather than down. I will have loud music or drumming playing in my car so that the energy levels are high. I use a song called 'I've Got The Power' by Snap, which everybody knows from the Jim Carrey film *Bruce Almighty*. Other mediums use other songs. I know one student who uses the James Brown song 'I Feel Good'. Whatever the song is, the key is to get yourself and your environment energised.

Spirit Truth: mediums get emotional

I know I am an unusual medium. I do a lot of things that go against the grain. One of them, for instance, is that I have fun and get emotional! I make no apologies for this because I find what I do incredibly rewarding. When I connect with spirit I have gone through the veil and I am partly there with them. And whenever I experience the Other Side, I enjoy it. As a result, I laugh and I cry when I demonstrate.

This is another area in which I seem to upset the conventional world of mediumship. According to the traditionalists, you aren't allowed to have emotions. But, to me, that seems completely wrong. Part of what I do is based on empathising with and understanding people's feelings. If, for instance, a child that has passed in tragic circumstances comes through, I will feel that intensely because I am a mother myself and I can imagine the pain. Now, of course, I wouldn't stand there and blubber and make it all about me. But when I experience that unconditional love people have for their loved ones coursing through my body, I am overwhelmed sometimes.

When you are sitting with a father who is talking to his son whom he absolutely adored and he is crying his eyes out, you can't help but be touched by it. You'd be a robot if you didn't cry with them. And I'm certainly not one of those.

I've had some remarkably emotional experiences during the course of my career. The atmosphere that spirit can create when it is coming through can be amazing. I've experienced moments when I've been demonstrating and everyone could feel the electricity in the room.

DRY YOUR EYES

One such occasion happened one night when I was working at a small theatre in Shrewsbury.

The energy within the room was great from the very beginning. Everyone in the audience seemed to be in the right mood. At one stage I got a message from a young man. He was a very gentle, warm and loving soul, I could tell. He was trying to communicate with two women, one a middle-aged lady and another younger lady, who were sitting in the front row. They turned out to be his mother and fiancée.

I could sense that the man had died in a tragic

accident. At first he communicated on a general level. He told them how much he loved them both, reassured them that he was all right and even apologised to his fiancée for a small tiff that they'd had before he passed. It was nothing really. One of those 'you didn't kiss me this morning' type arguments, but he knew that she'd been holding on to it and he wanted her to let it go.

The message wasn't actually that unusual. What was out of the ordinary, however, was the way that the emotions spread around the room.

The mother and the fiancée were very tearful during the message. I'd been quite upset myself and that had been clear to the audience. It was only when the man's energy began to fade, to be replaced by that of another man, that I realised how much of an impact the message had made on the audience.

I found myself being drawn to a lady in another part of the theatre. 'This man is coming through to dry your eyes,' I said. 'I have no idea what that means, but he is here to dry your eyes.'

'I know what it means,' she said to me. 'I've been crying my eyes out listening to that message. The spirit with you is my brother. He always used to dry my tears for me when I was upset as a little girl.'

That set me off and soon there were others dabbing away at their faces with handkerchiefs up and down the aisles. It underlined for me how powerful spirit can be in affecting each and every one of us. There are times when I think I should be sponsored by Kleenex.

Spirit Truth: **mediumship can be a laughing matter**

I'm not being disrespectful to the spirit world when I laugh and joke during my demonstrations. I am simply being true to it. That's because the spirit world is not full of grumpy people. It's full of people with a sense of humour.

As far as I'm concerned, there's something very reassuring and uplifting about a dad coming through to his family and making them laugh in the way that he did when he was with them in this life. It's genuine and real. I've communicated more than my fair share of funny stories over the years. A few stick in the memory more than most.

THE TICKING CLOCK

It was getting towards the end of an evening demonstration in Croydon and I was becoming increasingly frustrated by something. Throughout the evening I had been hearing the sound of a clock, ticking away in the back of my head.

I had no idea what it related to and had asked the audience whether it meant anything to anyone, but to no avail. A few times I'd been drawn towards a gentleman sitting with a couple of other people towards the front of the audience. I could tell immediately he was a 'dragged-along' and was really sceptical about what I was doing. But he wasn't reacting to anything I said so I'd had no option but to move beyond him.

As the demonstration drew to a close and I got a signal from the stage manager that I could only bring through one more message, I was drawn back to him again. By now the sound of the ticking clock had become almost deafening. I'd also been joined by the spirit of a man in his late forties, who was standing behind me. He was a very amusing character, a real Peter Pan, very young at heart despite his age. He was a Londoner, and had a really cheeky, Cockney personality.

As well as the ticking clock I started hearing the song 'Da Doo Ron Ron'. That suggested to me that his name was Ron – or Bill, from the line 'somebody told me that his name was Bill'. I picked up on some other things as well. For instance, I felt very strongly that he was trying to connect with his son. I could also smell fresh earth, which suggested to me he'd been buried – perhaps very recently.

No one was reacting to what I was saying, but I was certain that the object of this man's interest was somewhere in the audience. So I repeated it all again, this time looking at the face of the sceptical guy near the front. This time I saw a very different reaction. He was shaking his head and smiling. 'I don't believe this,' he said to a lady who was sitting alongside him.

There are times when you get an overwhelming sense

of something being right and this is what I felt now. So I asked him directly: 'This is your dad, isn't it?'

He just looked at me and grinned: 'Yeah, I know.'

It turned out the guy was, like his dad, a real Cockney. He told me that his father had passed very recently. 'We only plotted him this morning,' he said. That immediately explained the smell of fresh earth that I'd picked up. He told me that someone at the funeral had persuaded him to come along to the demonstration, which he'd done extremely reluctantly.

There was something very warm and quite amusing about him. We had a bit of banter and the whole audience was laughing, partly with joy at the communication that was happening here.

The only thing that I needed to clarify now was this ticking clock.

'As I say, I keep hearing the sound of a ticking clock,' I told him. 'It's been bugging me all night and it's louder than ever now. Do you understand that? Does that mean anything at all to you?'

'Yes it does, as it happens,' he said, shaking his head. 'But I don't know how you can hear it because we took the batteries out.'

I looked quizzically at him. 'What do you mean, you took out the batteries?' I asked.

He explained that his father had a clock that he always complained about. It was a battery-powered, modern clock that made a loud ticking sound. The son hated it too. 'It used to drive us all nuts,' he told me.

His father had regularly joked that he'd bequeath it to him when he died. So the son had thought he'd have the last laugh by placing it in his father's coffin.

'We put it in there the night before the funeral, last night,' he told me. It was the kind of joke his father would have really appreciated, he said.

Sure enough he was laughing as he stood behind me. 'Well, I can tell you that he thought that it was funny,' I told him.

It was a memorable message for all sorts of reasons. It was one of the quickest communications I'd received and also illustrated that you don't need to be a 'believer' to receive a message from the Other Side. But it also showed, once again, that humour is as much a part of the Afterlife as it is of this one. We should all take every opportunity to laugh together ...

FISH OUT OF WATER

As I have explained, I get all sorts of weird and wonderful messages, delivered to me in equally weird and wonderful forms. Few have been quite as weird and wonderful as the one I received a year or two ago while demonstrating in Ireland.

The moment the spirit of a very jovial, elderly man joined me on stage I knew I had a practical joker on my hands. Rather than offering me a string of names, feelings or even a piece of music that might help me identify and connect him with the audience, he began showing me something utterly bizarre – a giant fish! It was absolutely massive, the size of a horse, and was flapping animatedly in front of me. It was such a ridiculous and surreal sight that I couldn't help laughing and decided to share it with the audience, who were soon laughing along with me. I know next to nothing about fish and would struggle to tell the difference between a cod and a killer whale.

But all of a sudden the guy was giving me two words, which I shared them with the audience. 'I don't even know what they mean, but I'm being given the words koi carp,' I said. Again, this was greeted with waves of laughter around the theatre.

I was then given another image, of a man walking around this giant fish. He was stalking round it, looking nervously in all directions. It was as if he was a security guard, protecting the most valuable thing on earth.

Again, when I shared this with the audience they thought it was hilarious. Throughout all this, the spirit of the elderly man was having an absolute ball. He was laughing so loudly I burst into a fit of coughing at one point. After a while, however, I realised that there was a serious side to this, which I needed to address. It was all very entertaining, but if someone was trying to send a message I wasn't doing very well in interpreting and passing it on.

I had no idea where this was going and didn't really expect anyone in the audience to recognise the man from the information I'd given them so far. 'So does anyone understand this image of someone watching over a fish, or maybe a large number of fish?' I said, reaching out for some kind of reaction.

I was really surprised, not to mention relieved, when I saw an arm go up. It belonged to a guy in his late twenties, who was sitting a few rows from the front of the auditorium. He was wearing a sheepish smile and kept looking almost disapprovingly at the young woman next to him who had clearly made him put his arm up.

'Do you understand this?' I said, sensing that I had to be gentle with this guy.

'I do,' he said. 'I think you've got my father-in-law with you.'

The elderly man's demeanour changed at this point. There was still a smile on his face, but it was now warmer and more loving. He clearly thought the world of this young man.

The spirit now showed me some other images of the young man working in water. He was doing something that involved fish, feeding them and moving them around in a giant, almost industrialised, pond or lake.

He nodded at this. 'I work on a fish farm,' he told me.

I spent a few minutes passing on a message from the elderly man to his son-in-law. It turned out that the pair had teased each other relentlessly when the old man had been alive. He was from a generation of farmers who believed that farming was about looking after cattle and sheep. So when his son-in-law had got a job running a fish farm in the Irish countryside he had ribbed him mercilessly about it.

The son-in-law had taken all this in his stride. He knew fish farming was more profitable than old-fashioned farming in Ireland and that he was providing for his wife and young family. Deep down, he also knew his father-in-law was proud of him.

The images I was being shown related to a problem that the son-in-law had at that time. The farm bred Koi carp, an expensive tropical fish that people put in ornamental ponds in their gardens. The farm had been plagued by thieves who were regularly breaking into the grounds in the dead of night and draining the waters of their carp. This guy had tried everything he could to stop them – from CCTV to posting night watchmen round the pools where the fish were kept. But it hadn't solved the problem.

The young man's wife – and the spirit's daughter – wasn't in the theatre that night, having just given birth to a baby, this man's grandchild. I sensed that this was where the spirit's real interest lay. He was worried that her husband would do something silly that might cause her pain. By now he had stopped smiling and had become quite serious. He asked me to convey a few simple messages to his son-in-law.

'In all seriousness,' I said, 'your father-in-law is telling me that you need to stop worrying so much about these thieves. The police are involved and they will sort it out eventually. You've got a young family to look after and support. If you don't stop stressing about this so much you are going to have a nervous breakdown or suffer a heart attack. And what use are you going to be to your new baby if that happens?'

I could tell from the young man's demeanour that this was hitting home. He was nodding quietly and looking down at his feet. When the spirit began to fade and finally asked him if he understood what he'd said, the young man looked at me and said: 'Yes, I did, and he's right.'

Spirit Truth: you don't need to believe in mediumship and the spirit world in order to receive messages

---

THE SECURITY GUARD

Some people are genuinely unsettled by what I do. A few react to it quite violently. During the course of my career I've been called a freak, a witch – and worse. There have been times when I've wondered whether I'm living in the Middle Ages rather than the twenty-first century. But I accept that everyone is entitled to their opinion. It's a free world – here and in the Afterlife.

At the root of many people's attitude, I believe, is fear. They are afraid to accept that the spirit world exists and that those who have passed over can communicate with us. Some people will never overcome that fear. They will carry it with them to the grave – at which point, of course, they will be in for a big surprise.

A few, however, see the light as a result of meeting mediums like me. The transformation that comes over people when they face that fear and discover the truth can be a wondrous thing to behold. It's happened to me a few times. One of the most touching came when I was working at a Pontins holiday camp in the West Country as part of the British Mediums Weekend.

It's an event that I really enjoy participating in, partly because mediums spend a lot of time working in isolation and it's a nice opportunity to mix with the small group of gifted individuals who share my unusual profession. I also enjoy it because of the audiences, who are always lively and enthusiastic, something that helps me no end when it comes to summoning up communications from spirit, because spirits are drawn to positive energy.

On this particular Friday evening the atmosphere was even livelier than usual. Everyone in the large theatre was in the mood. Well, almost everyone.

Towards the end of the evening, I found myself in the presence of the spirit of a father. He was relatively young and had passed quite recently. I got the very strong sense that he had passed quickly and hadn't had the chance to say goodbye to his family. I got the feeling he was a fit man and his passing had been totally unexpected. It had hit his family hard.

As I began to pass on information, however, there was no obvious sign of a recipient for the message. The livelier members of the audience towards the front of the room were looking blankly at me, shaking their heads when I asked them whether the information I had meant anything to them.

Slowly but surely, I was being drawn towards the back of the room, which, unlike the rest of the space, was swathed in darkness. But there was no reaction there at all.

So I said: 'Is there somebody at the back that understands it?'

Suddenly, to my surprise, I saw a young security guard walk forward. He had been watching over the audience and the exits at the rear of the room and was clearly unsure whether he should be stepping into the spotlight like this. I could see the camp's manager standing nearby and threw him a look as if to say: 'Is this OK?' He smiled and nodded.

I asked the security guy to step forward a little more so that I – and the audience – could see and hear him better. He was in his early twenties and dressed in a smart uniform of white shirt, tie, blue trousers and blue jumper. He said his name was Steve. He wasn't the world's most communicative person.

'Do you understand all this?' I asked.

'Yes.'

'Do you recognise this as your dad?'

'Yes.'

I heard a slight murmuring sound in the front rows and could sense that the rest of the audience was finding this a bit boring so I decided to liven things up a little.

'So is it right that you just said to someone around the corner: "What a load of old rubbish, how long is she going to go on for?"' This drew an instant laugh from the front rows. Steve's face turned a deep scarlet and he looked down at the floor.

'You don't need to answer that,' I said, letting him off the hook. 'The crucial thing is, do you believe in it now, then?'

'Well I have to now, don't I, because that's my dad,' he said, drawing a ripple of applause from the rest of the audience.

I didn't want to prolong the poor guy's discomfort for too long, but his father had made a huge effort to get here so I passed on a few simple messages of love. He told his son that he was proud of the way he was conducting himself in his job – and in life. Steve stood there, nodding.

It was clear that the magnitude of what was happening to him was slowly sinking in. His body language was changing. He was becoming less resistant and more relaxed. Like so many people who have suffered during the loss of a loved one, Steve had clearly been bottling up his emotions. Now, finally, they were being released. By the end of the message he was openly crying.

When it was all over, his manager moved round to the back of the room to give him a consoling pat on the back and the audience showed their understanding with a healthy round of applause. Everyone in the room realised what a significant moment it had been for the young man, I think.

After the demonstration, as I sat and signed books and chatted to the audience, Steve wouldn't come anywhere near me. He stayed four or five feet away even though he was supposed to be protecting me.

'I thought you were meant to be making me feel secure, Mr Security Guard?' I teased him at one point.

'I'm not coming anywhere near you,' he replied with a gentle smile. By the end of the evening, however, he had summoned up the strength to sidle up for a brief chat. He told me his dad was a very sceptical and opinionated man. If he'd been in the room tonight he would have been just as dismissive of me as Steve had been initially.

'It must have been a hell of a shock to him when he passed over and realised that he'd been wrong about something all his life,' he smiled.

He told me that he'd given his mother a quick call on his mobile to tell her that a medium had connected him with his dad. She'd been very excited and had invited him round for dinner on his next night off so that he could tell her all about it.

I sensed that, as a family, they'd all been bottling up their emotions in the way that Steve had done. I was certain that they would have a lot to talk about.

There's nothing more rewarding for me, as a medium, than getting through to people like Steve, convincing them that there is something beyond this life, that our existence continues somewhere else after we have left this mortal shell. In many ways, it is my single most important purpose. I felt very proud to have helped him that night.

Spirit Truth: spirits connect in their own time

HE AIN'T HEAVY, HE'S MY BROTHER

Talking to people as I travel around the country and overseas, I'm always struck by how much confusion there is about spirits and their ability to communicate from the Other Side. Many people assume that it is a straightforward process for them. They can simply find a medium and get through to their loved ones in this world. They also assume that spirits want to come through and communicate. But it's not that simple.

Again, the easiest way to explain the truth of what is happening here is to compare this world to the Other Side. It makes a lot of sense when you think about it in this way. In this world, we know that some people are better communicators than others, while some people are less willing to push themselves forward. We all know people who are naturally chatty and happy to be in the limelight. And by the same token, we all know people who are more sensitive and who prefer to shy away from the spotlight.

So it shouldn't really be a surprise that shy and gentle souls from this life are often much the same on the

Other Side. They can be more reluctant to communicate, leaving others to bask in the attention. That was certainly the case with a lovely boy called Lee.

I first became aware of him when I was demonstrating to a small group of people in a hotel in Cardiff. Early on in the evening, I could feel the very faint energy of a young man. I could sense he hadn't been passed for very long and had left this life very suddenly. I could also feel that he was sensitive and quite reserved but also a very kindly and caring soul. He had soon made way for another boy who had died in a car accident and whose family was in the audience that day. I could almost feel the first spirit waving the second one through, telling him that he was more of a priority.

Afterwards I was signing books when I was approached by a lovely young lady who asked me to sign a photograph. When I looked at it, I was shocked. I recognised it immediately as the young man whose energy I had felt earlier but who had chosen not to come through. She felt a mixture of emotions when I told her this.

She told me her name was Charmaine and explained that the photograph was of her brother. She didn't tell me his name. On the one hand, she felt sad that he hadn't made a connection but on the other she was pleased when I explained that he had taken a step back because he had felt the other family were in more urgent need of hearing from their son. She said that was typical of him. He was a quiet, withdrawn person, but also one who thought of others.

I was able to tell Charmaine a little bit more. When I'd been in his presence earlier I'd got the distinct sense that his passing had been very quick. It was as if he had been here one minute and gone the next. I'd also felt a shortness of breath which could have been connected to a medical condition. I felt that since he'd passed over he was often in the presence of his mother, who missed him a great deal. I said I'd had the impression of him having a very large funeral, attended by a great many people. Charmaine nodded at all this and thanked me. She said she'd see me again, which a lot of people say. As it turned out, we did meet again – four years later, this time in Swansea, where she had booked a one-to-one session with me at a hotel there.

I was able to connect with her brother quite easily, which surprised me a little, remembering how sensitive he was. I was aware of the Hollies' song 'He Ain't Heavy, He's My Brother' when he arrived and, sure enough, he seemed a little more settled in the spirit world now and was able to share quite a lot of information with me. It was a very emotional sitting and I remember my eyes were often filled with tears, as were Charmaine's.

I was once more aware of the breathlessness I'd felt in Cardiff but this time I could also feel his heart racing. It was almost as if it was working twice as hard as it should have done. It was as if he had a forty-year-old heart in a twenty-year-old body, I told Charmaine, to which she nodded. I felt like he had died of a heart condition. I learned later that he had a very rare condition that only ten other children in the UK had. He had been treated for it at the famous Great Ormond Street Hospital in London.

He also showed me his funeral again, this time in more detail. I told Charmaine that it felt like Michael Jackson's funeral, the music was so loud and there were so many people there. I could see all sorts of bits and pieces inside his coffin and at the graveside. But I also saw some more intimate moments with Charmaine and her mother, as they said their goodbyes.

He also showed me images of his grave and the view around it. I could see statues of angels.

Once again, he was a little bit reluctant to take centre stage, so at one point he brought through another young man who had died recently. He was known to the family and passed on a message to Charmaine that she was to give to a friend of hers, Ryan.

Charmaine's brother didn't fade into the background on this occasion, however. As the sitting continued, he showed me two important things. One related to Charmaine and her children. I felt that Charmaine was worried that her children might have inherited the same condition as her brother and had recently taken them for tests in hospital. Her brother showed me that he had been there watching over them and was delighted that the tests had shown Charmaine's children were perfectly healthy and normal. She was very emotional at this news, as was I.

The other important piece of information related to his mother and the suffering she'd been through. She had been haunted by the fact he was born with the heart condition. She had blamed herself for this, even though there was absolutely nothing she could have done about it. The fact that he was born with the condition was a one in several million chance.

Being a mother, however, she never quite saw it that way.

Then, when he'd passed over, Charmaine's mum had been riddled with doubt about donating his heart to medical science in the hope that it would help others in the future. She'd agreed to do this but wondered about it every day of her life, asking herself whether she'd done the right thing. 'She thinks about it every night when she closes her eyes,' Charmaine confirmed.

I held her hands at this point and reassured her – and her mother – that they had done the right thing. Her brother told me he was pleased that they had done that and that it was helping others. That was a very emotional moment for Charmaine. It had been a very intense and very detailed sitting, with many more details that rang true for her.

What was interesting about it was that, throughout the sitting, her brother was reluctant to tell me his name. It was as if he was too shy to share it. I wanted to pass it on to Charmaine, however, in part to give her 100 per cent validation that it was her brother. At first I felt the letter D was significant. It turned out that was his nickname, Dodge. It was only at the end that I suddenly saw a sign saying Lee, as in the jeans. 'Who is Lee?' I asked Charmaine. She just smiled, wiping away the tears, and said: 'That's my brother.'

As we chatted after the sitting she told me that she'd been to a lot of events with other mediums but hadn't been able to make a connection with Lee. I told her I wasn't surprised at this. He was a shy and sensitive person, and not the kind of character to push himself forward. However, I said, it was clear that he was a person who cared for others, as he had proven on both the occasions I'd connected with him when he had helped others to come through ahead of him. But he was also still caring for his family on this side, watching over his mother, his sister and his younger relatives as well.

Charmaine was able to explain some of the things that I'd communicated to her, which hadn't quite made sense to me during the sitting.

I know the sitting was a huge comfort to Charmaine and her family because they wrote to me afterwards and have stayed in touch. The memory of Lee continues to inspire them and they are more proud of him today than they have ever been. And they have very good cause to feel that way too.

A WHOLE LOTTA LOVE

Spirits can make contact with us within moments of crossing over to the Other Side. I've had examples of people making contact with me less than an hour after they have passed. Some spirits, however, take considerably longer than this to come through to their loved ones. The emotion and sheer joy this produces in loved ones who have sometimes waited decades to make contact can be moving in the extreme.

I recently read for another medium, a very talented psychic and healer with whom I'd come into contact. Her name was Anna.

The moment I sat down and began, I sensed a family that had suffered a lot of tragedies. I kept seeing reports in local newspapers featuring the family. 'There have been too many headlines,' a young female voice said to me. It was the spirit of a young girl, Anna's daughter, Becky. She was a really vibrant, lively personality and had passed quite recently. I could sense that her passing had been very sudden and violent. Anna nodded at this.

'A car accident,' she said.

People imagine that mediums don't grieve. They seem to think that, because we have some kind of hotline to the Afterlife, we are immune from the pain and suffering that bereavement brings. That is so wide of the mark. If anything, I think, we feel the pain more acutely because we are so sensitive.

It was clear to me that Anna had suffered – and was continuing to suffer. She was trembling and close to tears as Becky shared her message with her.

The next image Becky gave me was the symbol for *The X Factor* tv show. For a moment I tried to interpret it as meaning something about an ex-boyfriend. When I told Anna this, however, she just smiled.

'No, it's exactly what you see. She was a really talented musician and was going to audition for *The X Factor*,' she said.

Within a few minutes, Becky's energy was beginning to fade. At first I felt as if this was going to signal the end of the sitting, but then I sensed another spirit was trying to come through. The first sign of his presence was the sound of a Led Zeppelin song, 'Whole Lotta Love'. It was accompanied by something else – a really powerful, burning sensation in my arm.

When I described this to Anna, she gasped. 'No,' she said, a look of complete shock on her face.

'You understand what this means?' I said.

'Yes I do, but I can't believe that it's who I think it is,' she said, becoming even more emotional now.

I felt myself in the presence of a teenage boy. He felt like a brother, but not to Becky. He felt more like Anna's brother. I was also hearing the name Clive.

Anna was by now reduced to just nodding.

Clive's first words were very clear – and very joyous. 'I am SO chuffed to be here,' he said.

Anna began crying at this.

He went on to tell her that he was happy where he was. But he also wanted to offer her some advice: 'Please stop mourning Becky. She is here with me and she is happy here. You can now start enjoying the fact that you know the two of us are at peace and together.'

We talked afterwards and Anna explained that Clive had died thirty years earlier. He had been playing near their home with some friends. They'd gone on to some kind of industrial site and had been climbing around it. Clive had been scaling a wall and had reached out to haul himself up. He had somehow picked up a live electric cable. He received a massive electric shock and died instantly.

Anna told me that his death was one of the reasons she'd become interested in mediumship and the psychic side of life. She had spent years desperately trying to establish some kind of contact with Clive. She'd detected his presence once or twice when she'd joined some circles run by Spiritualist churches. But there had never been any communication from him. To not only have heard from him, but to have been given such a wonderful and empowering message, meant the world to her.

It meant the world to me too, as it happens.

PART FIVE:
The Truth about Children and the Spirit World

'A child's spirit is like a child, you can never catch it by running after it; you must stand still, and, for love, it will soon itself come back.' *Arthur Miller*

Whenever I demonstrate publicly, whether it's at a church or a theatre or any other venue, I always try to find time to do a Q&A section in which people can ask me anything they like about my work and the spirit world in general. I find it's a great way to connect with and get to know my audiences and learn about what is important to them.

It probably won't surprise you to learn that the subject that I get asked about most often is children. The loss of a child is one of the most devastating things that we have to deal with in life and raises so many questions. What happens to a child when they pass into the spirit world? Do they grow up there? Are they reincarnated or do they remain in spirit so that they can communicate with their parents? What happens to unborn children?

As a mother, it's a subject that resonates really strongly with me. I'm fortunate in many ways. Because of the work I do, I have been able to pass on to my two sons the knowledge that life goes on after we pass on from this existence.

Even so, I feel very emotional whenever I deal with the spirit of a child or with parents who have recently lost a young one. In this next section, I will share some of the truths that I have come to know and understand during my years as a medium.

As I've said, I disagree strongly with the way that some mediums describe and explain the spirit world. One of the things that I object to most is the idea that children are somehow different when it comes to spirit communication. According to a (thankfully) small group of mediums, children can't communicate as spirits because they become reincarnated. This is plain wrong. I know it is because I have communicated with many, many children during my long career as a medium. Some of them are even spirit guides.

For instance, I have a young girl who works with me; she often comes through to help me communicate with other young people. This is one of the most important messages of all that I try to get across to grieving parents.

Their children can have a purpose in the other world as well. So sometimes when a child has been taken from you into the other world, it's because they have a purpose there. So you know that their life there – or their death here, if you like – has been given meaning.

Spirit Truth: **children are always cared for in spirit**

Another concern that many parents who have lost children carry with them is the fear that they are alone. This is, in some ways, one of the most upsetting things of all: the thought that a child, who has been cared for and loved in this life, has suddenly been cast adrift, left to its own devices. This concern is, of course, totally understandable.

The good news, however, is that my experience of the spirit world tells me that this simply isn't the case. As a medium, I have never had a communication from a child who hasn't acknowledged that there is a spirit adult with them too.

This isn't that surprising when you think about it. As I've said before, the spirit world is an extension and reflection of this world – or maybe it's the other way around! In this world, we simply don't leave very young children on their own. There are always people around to care for them, whether it's their parents, siblings, grandparents, aunts, uncles or nursery teachers. It's exactly the same on the Other Side. There is always someone at their side. It's one of the most valuable pieces of information I can pass on to the parents of children who have passed.

Spirit Truth: **the spirits of children age differently**

This leads to another common question: do children grow up on the Other Side?

Again, different mediums have different opinions here. The late, great medium Doris Stokes, for instance, always used to talk about the child that she lost, her son Stephen. She used to talk about how she dreamt that he was growing up in the spirit world. She believed that when she joined him he was going to be a grown adult.

I think she may well have been right about that. But I also believe there is no hard and fast rule and that it depends on the circumstances surrounding the passing of the child. As a result, they may appear to be at the same age as when they passed, or at the age they would now be if they'd remained in this life. So, for example, if they were twelve when they passed they may present themselves ten years later as a twelve-year-old or as a twenty-two-year-old.

Of course, many babies don't make it into this world at all. They die at birth or even before that. So what happens to them? Do they have an existence in the spirit world? Some of my experiences in mediumship have given me a few insights into this. So the best way to answer these questions is via a couple of the most revealing messages I've received.

THE DECEMBER BABY

A few years ago, I was touring with two of my closest colleagues in the world of mediumship, Colin Fry and Tony Stockwell. We were appearing together in the Best of British Mediums tour, playing to full houses at theatres all over the UK and Ireland. One day in the spring, we had just arrived in Dublin when we received some bad news. One of the tour managers, a lovely guy called Tony Lewis, had got a phone call from his partner Rachel, telling him that she had suffered a miscarriage.

It was devastating news for Tony and Rachel because this was their first pregnancy. They were both in their thirties and nervous about the whole thing. So to lose the baby like this, especially as it was early on in the pregnancy when they had just begun to tell people their exciting news, was terribly upsetting for them both.

Tony told me about Rachel personally. I gave him a big hug and wanted to shed a tear with him, but I couldn't because I had to share something with him. The moment he had passed on his news to me I got a very clear message in my head, which I repeated to him. It consisted of just four words, but they were very powerful ones. I told him: 'He will come back.'

There are times when being a medium is a real burden. You have to tell people truths that you'd really rather not have to tell them. Part of me hadn't wanted to share this with him. His emotions were too raw. Because Rachel's pregnancy had been still in its first trimester, they also hadn't known the sex of the child, so I felt like I was sharing too much information with him. But I knew I had to pass on the message. It didn't take long for me to understand why.

Tony and Rachel did the right thing and tried for another baby immediately. Sure enough, within a few weeks Rachel was pregnant again. They were understandably anxious about it so kept the news to themselves until much later in the pregnancy this time. This time, thankfully, the pregnancy was healthy although the baby – a boy they named Theo – did arrive extremely early and had to be cared for in hospital for a while.

It was only when I spoke to Tony and he explained to me what had happened that the truth hit me. 'Do you know the funny thing, Tracy,' he said. 'He arrived on December 17. That was around the date that the baby we lost was due to be born.'

The moment he said that I got an overwhelming sense of what had happened. It was as if the baby didn't make it the first time but then came back. Rachel needed to be his mum and Tony was meant to be his dad. He didn't make it the first time but he did the second time.

So when I said to Tony he will come back that's what it meant.

Spirit Truth: children have a voice in the next world – even if they didn't have one in this life

---

TWO FAMILIES

The road to becoming a medium isn't an easy one to navigate. The fact that I've made it to the point where I am today is down to the help and guidance I received from a few special people. Many of the most influential figures in my life have been fellow mediums, naturally. They have been wiser and more experienced heads who have passed on their knowledge.

But some of those who have opened my eyes to the workings of the spirit world have been clients, people for whom I have read regularly. Among these are a couple named Barbara and Ray, who have become almost like family to me.

Barbara came to me years ago, soon after Ray had passed over, and I began sitting for her at my centre. We'd become quite close – so much so, that when I was going through a really rough patch as a medium and was on the verge of quitting altogether, Ray had been instrumental in talking me out of taking that step. He chastised me for even thinking about turning my back on the spirit world. His words had helped give me the strength to go on.

I'd continued sitting for Barbara and her family over the years and had got to know her and their daughter Karen very well. They had continued to be a huge influence on me, never more so than when I made a particularly memorable connection.

One day as I connected with Ray I was aware of the spirit of a child with him. The boy was actually in his forties, but still his spirit seemed to be that of a child. I was shown an image of a pair of jeans with the name Lee on them. When I explained this to Barbara she became quite emotional.

'That's the son I miscarried,' she told me.

It turned out that she had miscarried in between their two daughters. The little boy, who she and Ray were going to call Lee, would now be around forty-three years of age. This confirmed what I'd been told already by my spirit guides. Children that pass over either remain the same age as when they leave this life or they continue to 'age' at the same rate they would have if they were still here.

The knowledge that Ray was having a spirit world relationship with the son she never held was immensely moving – and, of course, reassuring – for Barbara. She thought it was wonderful that, in effect, there were two families. On this side of life, she was living with her daughters, while on the other, Ray was enjoying an existence with their son.

But that wasn't the only aspect of how children exist on the Other Side that Barbara and Ray helped me understand. Some time later, I did a sitting with Barbara in which Ray was talking about a little girl called Millie. I got the name when he sang me the song 'My Boy Lollipop', which was sung by Millie back in the 1960s. At the time, Barbara had not had a clue what he was talking about. But when she came back to see me a few months later, she revealed that Karen had recently given birth to a little girl, whom she'd named Millie. Barbara hadn't even mentioned the sitting with Ray to her so the name had come about totally independently.

Again, it provided me with an important insight into children and their spirits. Millie's granddad Ray had known her in spirit before she was born, while she was in Karen's womb. I've since shared this information to comfort other parents who have lost children either stillborn or through a miscarriage. It's been a huge help to each of them.

Spirit Truth: **spirits can inspire as well as heal**

DANIEL, YOU'RE A STAR

Just as we have a purpose in this life, so we have a purpose in the next one too. For a beautiful little boy named Daniel, his mission in the spirit world was not just to heal the pain of the family he left behind but to inspire them to live a meaningful new life as well.

I first came across his family when I did a phone sitting. That in itself was something of a rarity because I don't do many phone sittings. I avoid them for a few reasons. It's partly that you don't know who is at the other end of the phone sometimes, but it's more to do with the fact that I care about my client's emotional wellbeing. Receiving a message from spirit can be a very profound and overwhelming experience. As a medium, you can never be sure what your client's reaction is going to be like. For that reason, I much prefer to be with the client in person in case I need to give them a Kleenex to dab away the tears or wrap a comforting arm around them. If someone gets upset after a sitting at my centre, for instance, they are welcome to stay and have a cup of tea and take their time until they feel ready to leave.

Sometimes, however, I make an exception, mainly if someone lives in a different part of the country, or, as is sometimes the case, has a reason to maintain their privacy. A lady who met the former criteria was Joanne, who lived in Lancashire and wrote to me in urgent need of a one-to-one sitting. It didn't take me long to understand why she was so anxious to talk to me.

Within moments of beginning my sitting for her I was in the presence of a little boy. At first he was a bit fidgety. He had sat really awkwardly, as little boys do, and had plonked himself on my knee. 'He is sitting on my knee and he has the boniest bottom I've ever felt,' I told Joanne.

I could hear the song 'Daniel' by Elton John playing in my head and the boy was showing me the number seven.

'I have a son called Daniel in spirit,' she said. 'But he isn't seven, he was six when he passed.'

'That's what he's telling me and he looks seven. Hasn't he just had a birthday?' I asked her.

'Yes, he would have been seven last week,' she said, already getting a little emotional.

For the next few minutes I focused on my connection with Daniel. He was one of the most beautiful souls I've ever encountered. He was like a shining light. It was clear to me immediately that he had been loved by everyone who knew him from the moment he entered this life. He may only have been here for six years, but there was no sadness in the life of this beautiful boy.

Joanne was clearly still emotional but was able to agree with this. 'That's right,' she kept saying. 'Everyone adored Daniel.'

The next sound I heard was a slightly confusing one. I could hear the noise of water but also the sound of something landing in water and then the really loud, slapping sound of something hitting a rock or a hard surface. I could also see a man in terrible distress.

Crying quite heavily by now, Joanne said that she understood this.

Daniel was able to pass on a message of love to his mother, sharing a few memories of his time here with her before fading away.

Afterwards Joanne spent a few minutes telling me a little bit more about his passing.

She told me that Daniel had died in the most unexpected and tragic circumstances. His father had taken him to a park near their home. It had been the first time father and son had gone to this particular park together and they had both been really looking forward to it.

But when Daniel started playing near a pond things went horribly wrong. He had jumped onto some stones and landed so heavily that it had triggered a sudden and completely unpredictable heart attack. He had died instantly.

I can only imagine what her husband must have gone through in the ensuing minutes as first he, then an ambulance crew, tried to revive Daniel. But their efforts were all in vain. Obviously this had been utterly devastating for Joanne and her husband. It was literally as if the light had left their life. Joanne had been in a very dark place for weeks since his funeral and could see no hope, no reason to carry on. She'd called me at the suggestion of a friend who had received a message via me at a demonstration I'd done up in Manchester. She thanked me profusely for the sitting and said she hoped to meet me one day.

It was a couple of months later when I met Daniel again. I was working out of a small office in Enfield at the time while I moved from my old centre in Waltham Abbey to a new one in Hertfordshire. One morning, a man arrived for a sitting. I didn't pay much attention to his name when he signed in, apart from the fact that his first name was Steve.

Within moments I was hearing the familiar strains of Elton John and was in the presence of the lovely Daniel once more. He appeared next to me this time, standing there and holding my hand as if he knew his bony bottom had been uncomfortable last time.

'This is really weird. It's just like a message I gave to someone called Joanne,' I said.

'That's my partner. Daniel is my son,' he replied.

I was taken aback temporarily as I remembered Joanne's telephone sitting and the fact she lived in Lancashire somewhere. But such was Daniel's charisma and sheer goodness that I had soon forgotten that. Some child spirits are very tentative and unsure of themselves. Daniel was the opposite: he was so confident in his communication. He had some lovely things to pass on to his father, with whom he'd clearly had a close bond. He told Steve that he still sat in the back of his car when he was driving and that he still wrote on the window when it was steamed up.

He kept showing me a blue picture, something on his father's phone, which Steve recognised. He left delighted that he'd made contact with Daniel.

A few months later I was working in Stockport, near Manchester. I was midway through an evening demonstration when I heard that familiar music once more and saw the radiant figure of Daniel standing next to me on the stage.

'I've been joined by a boy called Daniel who I've met before,' I told the audience. 'I'm not sure why he's come here tonight, but I will try to connect him with whoever it is he is looking for.'

It didn't take me long to discover the object of his attention.

'Hello, Tracy, we're over here,' a voice said halfway back in the auditorium. I looked towards the back of the theatre where I saw Steve sitting with a lady who I assumed must be Joanne. I was delighted to see them, of course, but it did immediately put pressure on me. I hadn't known they were in the audience – it was a big crowd. So I didn't want the audience to think they were some kind of plant, but at the same time I knew that, having given them so much information about Daniel, I needed to deliver something different to satisfy them.

Fortunately Daniel was very clear again. As on the previous occasions, he had a grandfather with him but didn't draw on him at all. The main thing he showed me that night was images of his parents' house in a real mess, as if it had been burgled. Drawers had been opened and rummaged through.

'He is telling me about the bad men who have taken your things, Joanne,' I said.

Joanne nodded. 'Yes, we were burgled last week. They took all my most valuable and precious jewellery,' she said.

What was interesting about the message that Daniel delivered that night was that, because he had already spoken to his parents about his death, he was now free to talk about life going forward. So he spent time talking to them about the way their lives were now heading, reassuring them that he was happy and getting on with his own existence. I saw them briefly afterwards and they seemed ready to take a big step forward.

I came across Daniel again a few months later. I was demonstrating with Colin Fry in Dunstable, later that same year. He stood alongside me and held my hand again. Steve and Joanne were there once more. This time I let Colin pass on a message for him.

Steve announced that, after having his sitting with me and then encountering Daniel again in Stockport, the two of them were now travelling widely to see mediumship at work. They were attending churches as well as theatres. What was so positive, however, was the fact that they went to these events not because they wanted to communicate with Daniel, but because they simply enjoyed being in the presence of spirit. Steve told me that Daniel had only appeared once in another venue but that it didn't matter to him and Joanne.

'We know that he is safe and we know this is the world that he is involved in now, so just to be near it is enough for us,' he said.

I was so proud and pleased for them that they'd been able to emerge from their grief and the terrible loss that they'd felt in their lives since Daniel's passing. That is the point of mediumship in many ways: to help people think of their loved ones as continuing to exist, and not be caught up in the idea of them being dead.

But most of all I was proud of Daniel, their extraordinary little boy, who was still bringing light into people's lives even though he was no longer physically with them. Of all the children I've met in spirit over the years, he is one of the most inspirational of all.

THE PEACEMAKER

There are times when the sheer noise that the spirit world is making in my head can be deafening. It's usually a signal that the message coming through to me is an important one, a communication that someone is desperate to pass on.

That was certainly the impression I got when I was demonstrating at the Beck Theatre in Hayes one evening. The sounds began to arrive as I was taking my break during the interval. I had headed back to the dressing room looking forward to a cup of tea and ten minutes of peace and quiet but those hopes had been quickly dashed.

Instead I'd started to hear the sound of car engines revving up in my head. It was almost as if I was on the starting grid of a Grand Prix race. The roaring sounds were deafening. Soon I was seeing images of really flashy cars. There were Ferraris, Lamborghinis, Porsches – you name it, they were there. It was as if they'd all been crammed into my dressing room.

There was no way I was going to shake these sights and sounds out of my head, so when I returned to the stage after the break, I told the audience that I'd have to skip the normal Q&A session to deal with this message.

By now I'd sensed the presence of a young man. He clearly loved cars, although he was making it plain that he didn't own any of these high-performance cars I was seeing. He just loved being around them, reading about them and watching them on television.

To help make a connection the young man started giving me some names. He told me that Adam was his father, Michelle was his mother and Stephen was his brother. Almost immediately I said that a hand went up. As it did so, I recognised a familiar set of faces. It was a family that I'd read for a few months earlier.

Jack had died in a car crash. As is so often the case, during the first sitting he'd concentrated on the fact that he had passed over safely and that he was at peace. This had been a huge comfort for the family, and for Michelle in particular, who was grieving badly over the loss of her son.

This time, however, Jack didn't want to talk about the past; he was much more interested in the here and now. He showed me another car, a beautiful, bright new white

Range Rover. 'How does he know that? I only picked it up from the garage last week,' Michelle smiled.

He talked about a tattoo that his brother, mum and sister had all had for him.

It was clear to me that Jack had been a very important member of the family. He was the glue that had kept it together in many ways. I got a sense that the family was in danger of falling apart. Sadly, that's what happened.

A few months later, Michelle and her daughter Sue came to see me for a sitting at my centre. It was a very intense sitting, once more with Jack. I could tell from Jack that there had been a lot of emotions within the family – both good and bad.

The good news was that his sister was pregnant. Jack kept teasing her about this and kept referring to the baby as Little Jack. The bad news, however, was that Michelle and Adam had separated.

The death of a child can often be the catalyst for the break-up of a relationship. Parents can retreat into their shells emotionally, blaming themselves or each other for the heartbreak they are suffering. It is a common story. This is what had happened here. Jack's absence from the house had been a factor as well. He had always been the peacemaker within the family. Without his presence, it had all fallen apart.

Michelle knew what a family boy Jack was and was really concerned that he would be upset about the separation. He told her that he knew about it and sympathised with her. I won't go into the details because they were private, but Jack said he understood who was in the wrong in the separation. This was really important to Michelle, who – understandably – was in quite a fragile emotional state. The knowledge that her son was watching over her was a great solace to her.

Some children are the peacemakers in the family, and they remain that way regardless of whether they are on this side of life or the other. Jack was one such child. His efforts to heal his family will continue for a long time to come, I am certain.

THE LITTLE PRINCESS

I have spent most of my adult life communicating with those who have passed over to the Other Side. I don't keep count, but it's a safe guess that during the course of my career I've probably connected with many thousands of spirits, of all ages, races, creeds, colours and backgrounds. It's no surprise that some have made more of an impression on me than others. In spirit, as in this life, some people are more charismatic, interesting and inspiring than others.

Over the years I have encountered several children who have made a deep and lasting mark on me. A few of them have helped me understand the spirit world in a new and enlightening way. One of them was a young girl I met while I was demonstrating at the Grand Theatre in Swansea in 2011.

She made her presence felt quite early on during the evening. The moment I sensed her I could tell she was a very nice, intelligent young girl. She was quite a bubbly, warm personality. In contrast, however, the events she was describing to me were absolutely horrific.

I have a variety of gifts, one of which is clairsentience. It's a long word but its meaning is pretty simple: I can feel things. When I am in the presence of spirit I can feel an event or a memory that is being shown to me by thought or images. People often ask me what this is like and the best way to describe it is that it's like being deeply absorbed in a movie on television or at the cinema. When you are 'into' a movie in that way, you can often feel the emotions that are being displayed on screen, whether it is sadness or terror or happiness. It doesn't mean you are feeling it physically.

And it's the same with clairsentience: whilst you don't feel the same extremes of pain, you do get a sense of what the spirit who underwent that experience was going through at the time.

As my communication with this girl deepened, I underwent quite a profound clairsentient experience. I was able to see her in a wooded area and feel the terror coursing through her body as a young man attacked her. She was trying to get away from him, but was unable to do so. I felt her being beaten relentlessly with a stone or a brick. I could feel sharp pains in the head and then a sense of her slipping away as she lay alone in the woods.

All these images came quickly, as if they were being fast-forwarded. I got the distinct impression that the girl had shown me this primarily to help identify the people she wanted to speak to in the audience. To help me further, she gave me a name, Sonia, and showed me an image of her brother and sister. The detail I had been given was so specific and dramatic that I would have been amazed if I hadn't found the object of her interest almost immediately. Sure enough, I'd soon been drawn to a mother called Sonia and her two children sitting in the auditorium.

I got the strong sense that the girl had passed quite recently. Given the brutality of her death, I could understand why her mother, brother and sister were in the audience. It was a senseless killing and must have left them confused, angry and devastated. I found myself thinking that if that had been my child, I'd want to know the answer to so many questions. Was she traumatised by her death? How much was the memory of her killing holding her back in the Afterlife? How did she feel about those that she'd left behind? Did she somehow blame them for her passing? As the connection continued, she answered many of these questions.

By now I'd identified the girl as Rebecca, or Becca. Having successfully used the details of her passing to help me identify her and connect with her family, Becca didn't want to talk about the murder itself. This immediately told me that she was a spirit that was already developing well on the Other Side. She didn't want to dwell on the past, which answered one of her mother's questions immediately.

Instead she wanted to talk about the future – and in particular the future of the relatives she had left behind.

I sensed that her family called her their little princess and it wasn't hard to see why. Becca was a really clever girl and had wanted to be a lawyer. In fact, her ambition was to become a barrister. There was no reason why that couldn't have happened if she'd lived as she was very good at school.

One of the main things she wanted to get across was that she didn't want her failure to fulfil her potential to be repeated by her brother and sister. They were bright children too and she wanted to encourage them to work hard and strive for their dreams.

It was a very inspiring message. Everyone in the audience was deeply impressed by the fact that Becca was less interested in the fact she'd been murdered than she was in the reality that she had a loving family that needed pointing in the right direction after suffering a terrible loss. Yes, something awful had happened to their family, but there was hope, and life still goes on. Rebecca's life here might have come to an end, but their lives lay ahead of them.

It was, as you can imagine, a very emotional message. Her mother was still feeling a very raw pain. Her daughter's passing was an open wound for her. Her brother and sister were suffering badly too. But I felt that the message Becca had passed on had been a positive one for all of them.

The memory of her lingered in my mind all the way up the M4 as I headed back home the following day. It was when I arrived at my house that something unusual happened. I had headed down to Wales almost immediately after returning from a holiday abroad. So I'd not seen my post for a couple of weeks. I'd also avoided the news on TV and the radio.

When I got into my office I started to go through it all and discovered a copy of the *Daily Express* newspaper that a journalist had sent me. She had interviewed me for the paper and wanted me to see the piece that she'd written. It was quite a nice piece, as it happens. She wasn't the usual, sceptical media person that I was so used to encountering. After reading it, however, I flipped the page and – to my amazement – saw Becca's face staring out at me.

It was in a news report on the court case in which her murderer had been jailed. The details within the report were, if anything, even more awful than I'd imagined.

Her killer was a former boyfriend called Joshua. He was just sixteen and was given an 'indeterminate' jail sentence with a minimum term of fourteen years before he'd be considered for parole. The two had been sweethearts but, it appeared, he was prone to angry outbursts and had told friends that he 'hated' her. He'd coolly lured her to a spot in the woods near where he lived so that he could beat her to death. What was incredible was that he'd done so for a bet! A mate of his had bet him he couldn't carry out a cold-blooded killing and that he'd buy him a breakfast if he did do it. A breakfast?! How utterly depraved and sick is that?

Reading the report brought back a wave of emotions from the previous night. For a brief moment I was back in that wood with Becca. But it also made me feel glad that I'd successfully conveyed such an important message to Becca's family. It was clear to me now that part of the peace I'd felt around her was down to the fact that she felt there had been justice. Her killer had been caught and sentenced to many years in prison. Safe in that knowledge, she wanted her mother, brother and sister to pick up the pieces now and get on with their lives, knowing that she was safe, at peace and beginning a new existence in spirit.

As the day wore on, however, I couldn't help dwelling not just on her case but on those of other murder victims. It was something that had intrigued me for a long time. For years I had been connecting with spirits who had been taken in horrific ways, especially when I was doing the TV series *Psychic Private Eyes*.

Becca was similar to many of them. In fact, all of them had been quite calm, almost serene presences. I'd never had an experience where someone who was murdered had come back and said: 'I'm not secure, I'm not happy, I'm not OK.' I'm not saying they were pleased they had passed, but they weren't stuck in the memory of it like a lot of people imagine they are. Far too many people believe that, I think.

Becca had once again proven that point. When someone is murdered or dies violently, people assume they are still in pain, that they are somehow 'scarred' for eternity. That is simply not the case.

It made me want to know more, so in a circle later that evening I asked one of my spirit guides about the circumstances that surround violent death. I asked him how best to describe what happens. His answer was one I will never forget.

He told me that a death of this kind is, in many ways, the mirror image of birth. When a baby is born it is very painful to the mother. You can't really describe that pain to anybody, it's so intense. But the minute the baby is born that pain has gone. It's disappeared and become a memory of which the child is the product.

This is what happens to people who suffer violent or extremely painful deaths, my spirit guide Luke told me. At death, it is as if the person has been born, or reborn, into the spirit world. Because of that there are no mental scars as a result of the passing.

It was an important piece in the ever-evolving jigsaw puzzle that is the truth about the Afterlife. Becca had played a special part in cementing that knowledge for me. And for that, I'd always be grateful to her family's little princess.

A BOY CALLED AUSTIN

The impact a message from the spirit world can have on a person's life should never be under-estimated. As a medium, I am constantly being reminded of how even the simplest of communications can transform – and even save – the lives of people who have been devastated by a loss. It provides them with relief, comfort and, perhaps most importantly, hope at a time when all three of those things are in very short supply.

Someone who got all of these things – and more – from a message was a young man whom I'll call Tony. I met him one evening at a demonstration on the south coast of England. It had been a fairly typical gathering. The theatre was almost full, with around 300 people in the audience. I'd just returned to the stage after the interval. As usual, I'd chosen this moment to give the audience an opportunity to ask me questions. I looked out into the auditorium and saw a man in his early twenties put his hand up. I immediately found this quite unusual. A lot of the young men who come along to my performances are what I call 'drag-alongs'. They aren't particularly interested in what I do and have literally been dragged along by their wives or girlfriends.

This young guy was clearly not a 'drag-along', however. He looked a little nervous but he overcame his anxiety and took the microphone. 'I just wanted to know something. Are children able to communicate from the spirit world?' he said. It was a simple enough question, and far from an original one. I'd been asked it a hundred times before.

The answer to his question was, of course, a resounding *yes*. In this instance, however, he didn't just have to take my word for it. The spirit of a child was there to tell him in person.

Within moments of starting to talk to Tony, I had seen a little, dark-haired boy sitting on his shoulders. He had his legs wrapped around Tony's neck as if he was ready to be carried out on a walk. He was being very affectionate and was leaning down, kissing the side of Tony's face. It was pretty clear to me that this little boy was Tony's son.

Normally I wouldn't connect a spirit directly with a person who has just asked a question. I avoid it for my own protection more than anything else. If I did that, then everyone would be fighting to ask questions, knowing that they were going to get a connection. I'd never ever finish a demonstration. But in this case I felt I needed to make an exception. So I began to explain to Tony what I was seeing.

'I have got the spirit of a little boy here. He's actually sitting on your shoulders right now, wriggling around, leaning over and rubbing his face against yours,' I told him.

I will never forget his reaction. For the first few seconds his face froze in a look of absolute disbelief. Then the penny dropped – and his face lit up like Regent Street at Christmas. He was over the moon.

I was able to find out a little bit more about the two of them, and about the boy's mother, who was sitting next to Tony. The boy's name was Austin and he had died after a long illness.

At one point I could hear the music from an advert I'd once seen for the Great Ormond Street Hospital.

When I asked Tony if this meant anything to him he nodded. 'Yes, Austin spent a lot of time in there,' he told me.

I was slightly puzzled by the fact that Austin wanted to connect only with his father. His mother was there too and was clearly moved by what was going on. But then he showed me an image of Tony sitting desperately alone on a seafront.

At that moment I realised that Austin had a more serious message for his father. From the images I'd been shown I was pretty clear that Tony had been asking himself whether he wanted to be here any more. Austin was his first child and, as I could see, father and son had been totally devoted to each other. Losing his precious little boy had been absolutely devastating to Tony.

In the past few weeks he had begun giving up.

I could sense that Tony and his partner were having big trouble in their relationship. This was, of course, typical in a couple who had suffered such a loss. I doubted whether they would be together for much longer.

I was concerned and wanted to know a bit more about Tony and Austin, and indeed about Austin's mother. Fortunately they were linked to someone else sitting near to them who was familiar to me. Her name was Julie, and she too had lost a son at a young age. Her boy Jordan had come through to me previously and she'd visited me for private sittings.

Talking to her afterwards I discovered that Austin and Jordan were cousins. My first thought was that their family had been through an incredible amount of grief. To lose one child is distressing enough, to see two young lives ended so young must have been traumatic for everyone.

Through Julie I was introduced to Tony and established a way of staying in touch. I was really glad I did so.

He told me that Austin had been a very poorly little boy who had been through a lot of operations. It was clear that he had been here for a lot longer than he might have been if he had not had such amazing medical care and attention.

I could tell Tony that Austin was now with his cousin and his granddad. The young father's reaction was fantastic.

It's always been my policy when I encounter people who are going through such difficult periods in their life that I keep in contact. It's not that I want them to come and have a lot of sittings with me. I simply see it as part of my duty as a professional medium. If I've opened up that kind of dialogue, I feel it's only right to keep it going, even if it's only the odd message on Facebook or a phone call. That's what I did in the case of Tony.

Sadly, as I had sensed it would, his relationship

with Austin's mother didn't survive. The pain that Austin's passing had caused his parents was too great. Unfortunately, it's a story I hear far too often.

However, Tony not only survived the break-up; he thrived in the wake of it.

I knew that the message he'd received from Austin had been a life-changing moment for him. It had, in many ways, restored his relationship with his son. Sure enough, in the months and years that followed, he became a passionate fundraiser for Great Ormond Street Hospital, the institution which had done so much to give Austin those precious extra years. Without those years he'd never have got to know what a special boy Austin was. He promised that he would never forget the debt he owed them for that – and has lived up to that promise.

I regularly see notices that he has posted on Facebook asking for support for his latest run or walk or charity event. That simple message I passed on to him has given him a new purpose and meaning in his life. Austin's legacy is a very beautiful one.

Spirit Truth: all spirits are capable of communicating, even if they didn't do so in this life

---

A common misconception I come across is that we carry our disabilities into the next life. I've come across many people who believe this – that if, for instance, you were disabled in this life then somehow you will be disabled in the next one too.

I'm always surprised when I hear this because, to me, it's obvious that this isn't the case. The beauty of being released from this human body is that we are free to express ourselves purely in the form of thoughts and feelings. We no longer need to do things in a physical way. So, no matter what burden you carried in this life physically, you are released from it when you pass over.

I've communicated with many spirits who have confirmed this for me. One of the most memorable – and beautiful – of these spirits was a little girl named Mia.

BROWN-EYED GIRL

Many people think that our sole purpose is to live a full and happy life in this world. That's not always true. In my experience, it's also the case that some souls are born to find that fulfilment and happiness on the Other Side. For them, this life is merely preparation, a stepping stone on the way to a more meaningful existence. Few of the spirits I've encountered have exemplified this as profoundly as Mia.

I encountered her one day at my home, where I was temporarily doing sittings while I waited for my new centre to open a few years ago. I tried to avoid inviting people to my home if I could. I liked to keep work and private life separate. But when I got a call from an Indian family asking to see me, something told me I needed to make an exception.

On the day of the sitting, I opened the door to see a well-dressed and very polite, early-middle-aged couple. They were slightly withdrawn and I could tell they were nervous so I spent a little time putting them at ease.

Almost immediately I began the sitting I felt myself in the presence of a very young girl. The first thing I was aware of was her eyes; they were a beautiful brown. I could hear Van Morrison's song 'Brown-Eyed Girl' playing ever-so-faintly at the back of my mind. The moment I began to describe her, the mother's face began to brighten. She didn't say much, but was nodding affirmatively as I brought forward more evidence.

I could tell that the little girl had suffered during her time here. Her mother nodded at this. I could also tell that her passing had left her parents, and her father in particular, traumatised. I sensed that he'd not been able to say goodbye to her properly.

She then began to show me details of her bedroom, a pretty room filled with lovely toys and soft furnishings where she'd clearly been very happy. She went on to show me something else – her coffin. I will never forget it. It was stunning. It was white and her grandmother had put rose petals and prayer beads inside it. I saw her lying there and she looked like a beautiful china doll. She was wearing a gorgeous white party dress. It was like something out of *Snow White*.

The message she wanted to pass on to her parents was quite simple. She wanted to thank them for all the love and care they had given her. She also told her father not to worry about the fact that he'd not said goodbye. The most important thing she needed to tell them, however, was that they needed to carry on their lives without her and have a new family. She knew that they wanted to have another child but were worried about it. She told them they should go ahead and enjoy the experience of being parents again because they were so good at it.

As I spoke I could see a huge weight lifting off their shoulders. The wife was in floods of tears by the end and they were holding each other tight.

Afterwards her parents told me a little more about their little girl. Her name was Mia. Mia was very severely disabled from birth and was only able to communicate using her eyes. She suffered from a rare condition which meant that she would pass out and need to be resuscitated, sometimes in hospital. Her family were constantly on edge about her. They knew that one day she might not return to consciousness after passing out. So it proved when she was just four years old.

Mia had come home after being at a friend's birthday party. She'd dressed up in a beautiful party dress and had a wonderful time. But she was very tired when she got home and passed out soon after. Her father wasn't around but her mother was. She dialled 999 and asked for an ambulance. Sadly, it arrived too late. Mia had passed over before the medics could get there to resuscitate her.

What was interesting to me, as I thought about it afterwards, was how much more information Mia had been able to give her parents since her passing. During her life she had been unable to communicate at a deep and meaningful level with her parents. They couldn't have the kind of simple, day-to-day conversations that parents and their children normally have. Mia never told her parents about her friends at school, her favourite television programme or what she wanted for Christmas. She'd communicated very simply with her mother, mainly through those big, brown eyes. Just because someone can't speak, it of course doesn't mean they can't still have thoughts. That part of you hasn't been disabled. It is the same when someone has a stroke – the thoughts are there; the person just can't articulate them verbally.

Mia was not meant to be here for a long time. Her parents knew that. To have had four years was a bonus, given the number of times they'd nearly lost her. It had been longer than expected. But that time provided Mia with the opportunity to learn a lot that she could communicate from the Other Side. She was aware of who her parents were, what her bedroom looked like, she was aware that she'd been at that birthday party that day. So when she came through to me she was bursting with feelings and emotions that she wanted me to convey to her family.

It was, in many ways, one of the most beautiful, uplifting and liberating messages I'd ever passed on.

They were quite clearly wonderful parents and had give Mia all the care and love she could possibly have wanted. I could tell that her father had been haunted by the fact he wasn't present at her death, but she'd lifted that load off his shoulders. The fact that she had also told them she wanted another child to experience that love was extremely moving. I will never forget her – or her parents.

TEARS IN HEAVEN

I rely a lot on music to help me interpret messages I'm being sent by the spirit world. Hearing the sound of familiar songs often provides the vital link I need to understand and connect people on this side to their loved ones on the other.

Music can be very emotive and poignant, so it's no surprise, I suppose, that I've made some extremely touching and moving connections in this way. Few musical connections were as emotional as the one that I made one evening when I was demonstrating in Worthing on the Sussex coast.

I'd been on stage for about half an hour and had already brought through a couple of communications. Suddenly, all I could hear was the soft guitar and gentle melody and words of Eric Clapton's song 'Tears In Heaven' playing in my head. It is, of course, a really poignant song at the best of times. Clapton wrote it following the death of his young son, Connor, who died in incredibly tragic circumstances when he fell from an apartment block in New York. But when I became aware of a little boy standing alongside me the hairs on the back of my neck stood on end.

The little boy couldn't have been more than a year old. He was holding my hands in his. He had little chubby hands, I remember that vividly. Some people don't believe that their babies can come through because they've never had a physical communication with them in this life. But even tiny infants are capable of getting their message across.

The music continued to play, but as it did so I was also shown some images. They were a mixture of X-rays and diagrams. I'm no doctor but I could make out that the images were of lungs. I could also make out that they were upside down.

I began to share this information with the audience. I knew I had to tread carefully here so I was quite precise with my language. I was soon being drawn to a young couple, in their late twenties or early thirties. When I asked them if they understood what I was talking about, they nodded. They seemed quite nervous so I tried to make them feel at ease. It was their first child, a baby boy called Ross. His lungs hadn't formed properly when he was in the womb, which was why he'd passed at only one week old. He had not been gone for long, only a few months, so their pain was still very raw.

Yet they were delighted to receive their baby's message. I spoke to them afterwards and they told me they hadn't believed that Ross would ever come through to them, mainly because he hadn't developed enough to communicate with them. So I explained that babies can continue to grow in the Afterlife, which came as a huge release and relief for them.

As I drove home in the car that night, Eric Clapton's song came on the radio. I couldn't help but shed a tear or two myself, I have to admit.

PART SIX:
The Truth about Suicide and Other Violent Deaths

Another common misconception that people have about the Afterlife is that people are punished for being bad on this earth. This ties in with religion, of course. The idea of being banished to hell for your misdeeds in this life is an ancient one. But in my experience it's simply not the case. In this section, I will share a few experiences and thoughts on this difficult subject.

Spirit Truth: we aren't punished for our bad behaviour in this life

---

A year or two ago I held a sitting for a lovely lady called Sara. She'd lost her son Kurt in tragic – and controversial

– circumstances that were still shrouded in mystery long after his passing. Kurt had been a quiet, big-hearted boy but his life had been changed when he witnessed his father dying in a motorbike accident when he was just twelve. He'd fallen into a downward emotional spiral after that, starting to hate the world and attack everyone who loved him because he couldn't cope with the sadness and hurt he was feeling. As a result of this, his relationship with Sara became extremely strained.

Then, when he was seventeen, Kurt himself was involved in a fatal car accident. He was the passenger in a stolen car when it came into contact with a police car. According to the official reports, the police car had chased the stolen vehicle. The driver had lost control of the car, crashing into railings and killing himself and Kurt.

The loss had devastated Sara, who was convinced that there was something wrong with the police's account of the accident. She started conducting her own investigation, looking at CCTV tapes, inspecting the crash site and talking to people. But whenever she tried to present an alternative case she had the door slammed in her face and was told she was wrong. No one would listen to her, and as a result, she began ignoring everyone as well. She stopped trusting people and fell into the same sort of downward spiral that Kurt had experienced.

Fortunately, however, she did trust me. She had been to a few of my demonstrations and asked for a private sitting with me.

When we sat down the first person to come through was her father. She didn't particularly want to see him, but I told her that he was paving the way, helping the rest of her family on the Other Side to build the energy needed to bring Kurt through. Sure enough, Kurt soon connected with me.

She told me later that she'd been surprised at how calm and peaceful she'd been when he made contact. 'I thought I would be a crying wreck,' she admitted. Kurt told his mother how much he loved her and how sorry he was about what had happened between them.

Eventually, she asked me to ask him the question she was burning to find the answer to: what had happened on that fateful night?

Kurt showed me the scene and I saw that it was not the driver of the stolen car that had caused the accident, but the police car itself. It had been parked off the road and had driven out in front of the boys, forcing them off the road and into the railings.

It was at this point that Sara burst into tears. She felt a mixture of emotions: relief that she was right, anger at the cover-up and anguish again that she'd lost her son.

'What does Kurt want me to do now?' she asked me. 'I've been fighting this for ten years.'

His reply was one of the most moving I've ever relayed to someone. 'He says that you must stop now and put the lid on the black and white box that you have at home,' I said. 'You have done all you can and he doesn't want you to suffer any more. You both know the truth now and that is enough.'

Sara later told me that the sitting had changed her life. 'Without it I know I would still be here fighting and killing myself, wanting and demanding the truth.'

Just as Kurt had described, she did have a large black and white box in the living room at home containing all the newspaper reports, police files and correspondence that she had collected in her fight to prove Kurt's innocence. She told me that she had locked it away immediately. In time, she was sure, she would destroy it.

Of course, she still missed her son; what mother wouldn't? But receiving that message and knowing that Kurt wasn't suffering or in any way paying for his painful departure from this life had allowed her to take a big step forward. More than anything it allowed her to find a kind of peace.

Spirit Truth: **suicide victims are cared for on the Other Side**

A very common question that I am asked when I demonstrate relates to suicide. For some reason, many people believe that those who take their own lives are somehow dealt with differently from those who die from natural causes or in accidents that are beyond their control.

I suppose a lot of this thinking is influenced by religion, which teaches that suicide is a negative and selfish act. According to some faiths, those who follow this path are condemned to eternal damnation. In the Jewish faith, those who commit suicide are buried separately. To the Catholic Church, it is a mortal sin because in their view the decision to end a life should be God's choice and no one else's.

There's also a lot of negativity attached to suicide by some mediums. One so-called 'rule' says that if you commit suicide, then you can't connect with this world again until you have reached the age that you were supposed to live to. So, for instance, if you committed suicide at the age of fifty but were supposed to live naturally to the age of eighty, then people here wouldn't be able to communicate with you for thirty years. You would be stuck in some kind of limbo throughout that period, unable to do anything. How does that work? It makes no sense.

I have a slightly different opinion about the whole issue, one that is based, again, on my experience. Suicide is, without question, a very sad way to pass, one that causes many people an incredible amount of distress. But at the end of the day the spirits who pass in this way are going home. They are going back to spirit, where they are going to be nurtured and looked after. They are also going to be beginning the next part of the journey of their soul. There is always a reason why suicide victims have made their choices. In some cases,

I believe, they have made that choice because they feel they belong in the spirit world more than they do in this world.

I have encountered the spirits of many people who have committed suicide over the years. Each one has taught me something.

SISTER ACT

I was on stage in Swansea one night when I felt the presence of a young man coming through to me. It was obvious to me early on that he had taken his own life. I've been in the presence of many suicide victims before. They carry a different weight with them. Sometimes they are lighter; they feel as if they never wanted to be on this side of life. It's as if they are more comfortable and better-suited to existence on the Other Side.

That was not the impression I was getting about this young man at all, however. I got a very strong sense that it had been a spontaneous suicide, it had not been premeditated. He had simply snapped. His passing was also quite recent, within the last three weeks to a month, I felt.

I was able to make out his name. He was called Mark and I could feel that there were quite a few people in the audience with whom he had a family connection. I was able to identify them quite quickly from the information that I'd provided. His mother and sister were there and were quite emotional about hearing from him.

It wasn't a lengthy communication. Because he was a relatively new arrival on the Other Side that wasn't unusual. He was still adjusting to existence there and had made the effort to get through tonight mainly to pass on the vital news that he was safe and at peace. He also mentioned that he was spending time with his grandfather there, something that was very reassuring for his family. But that was about it.

That was fine, of course. Sometimes spirits pass on the equivalent of lengthy emails, other times they pass on brief text messages. Mark was passing on one of the latter. It was short and, as far as his family was concerned, very sweet.

There was something unusual about him, however, something that I'd never encountered at that time, especially in a suicide victim. He had company.

The other presence had been a peripheral one while Mark had been connecting with me, but it was clear to me that she was female. At first, I had a strong sense of the word 'sister'. Briefly, I thought it might be his sibling, but I soon decided she wasn't related to him. I then began to wonder whether the woman was another kind of sister, a nun. She had that kind of peaceful, caring personality to her.

As I tapped into her energy – and that of Mark – however, the penny finally dropped. I saw that she was a nurse, a nursing sister. This was underlined by the fact that of Mark's many family members in the audience, some were nurses in the NHS.

Until that point, I'd never seen someone who had committed suicide accompanied by someone else when they came through to me. It was clear to me that she was caring for him, helping his rehabilitation or rebirth in the spirit world. She was acting just like a nurse would in this life, in many ways. If a patient wanted to go out for a walk as part of his rehabilitation in this life, there's a very good chance that his nurse would accompany him to make sure that he was OK. That's what was happening here. Mark was venturing out during his rehabilitation in the spirit world and this nurse was with him.

In its own way, Mark's message that night was as profound for me as it was for his family. I learned something very powerful: that spirits are cared for and nursed on the Other Side.

TOGETHER

I was on stage in Swansea when I felt myself in the presence of a young man called Alan. From the energy he was sharing with me, I could tell that he had been around twenty-five when he had passed and that he had died in mysterious circumstances.

At first his message was pretty straightforward. Alan connected with his mother, who was in the audience, passing on his love to her. But as the message continued I could tell that he was more interested in the figure who was sitting next to her, dressed in a nurse's uniform. It turned out she was his cousin Katrina. And he had a message for her.

Alan showed me a succession of images which made it clear to me that he had been training as a nurse himself. For whatever reason, he had not made it. He told me that Katrina was going through the same training, but she was struggling with her studies. And it was clear that the loss of Alan had played a big part in that situation. He told me that he felt she was giving up her dreams. She had lost her confidence and was no longer the same motivated ambitious young women he had known.

She nodded quietly when I shared this information with her. Until that point, it was still a fairly typical message. I passed on communications like this on a regular basis. But having passed on this message to his cousin, rather than fading, Alan remained in place. At the same time he was joined by the spirits of four more young men. I got the strong sense that they had all taken their own lives – except for Alan. There was something less clear-cut about his case.

They kept repeating that they were not alone. 'We needed to be together,' they said. As I brought through more evidence, I discovered that there were others in the audience with connections to these young people. And as this evidence strengthened, I began to see that the link was the community from which each of them came: the Welsh town of Bridgend, where a number of young people had been committing suicide.

The spate of seeming inexplicable deaths had devastated the community, leaving a string of baffling questions. Why were these young people taking their own lives? Was there some kind of pact between them? What sort of conversations had they had with each other? Did they believe in some kind of reunion in the Afterlife?

The police and the media were nowhere near getting answers to any of these questions. But as I listened to these young people on stage that evening, I came to one very clear conclusion: many people imagine the Afterlife as a solitary experience. They think of their loved ones as lost and lonely souls. But this is not the case at all. Spirits group together in all sorts of ways. The most common groupings are families, whether it be parents and their children, brothers and their sisters or husbands and their wives. But in a lot of circumstances, spirits are drawn together by common experiences they have undergone in this life. This is particularly the case when a great deal of healing needs to be done.

The young people of Bridgend had come together in exactly that way. Whether or not they had intended to be reunited in this way we may never know. But what I do know is that they had all found some kind of peace on the Other Side. And I also know that discovering this was a huge consolation for their families and friends.

Spirit Truth: those who suffer traumatic or violent deaths don't suffer on the Other Side

---

A subject I'm often asked about is people who have left this life in painful or traumatic circumstances. I often meet the families of murder victims, for instance, who want to know whether the pain of the loved one's passing has somehow scarred that person in the spirit world. Those left behind are understandably anxious to know that the suffering comes to an end when their loved one passes over.

It's easy to see why they fear that their loved ones might be carrying some kind of burden through eternity. The common perception of 'ghosts' and troubled spirits is of people who have suffered at the hands of others and want some kind of revenge. If you believe some of the more sensationalist psychics and mediums, these poor souls are drifting around the Afterlife obsessed with the final moments of their earthly life. In my opinion, this is complete rubbish.

As I have said before, I believe that the pain we experience as we cross over from this life to the Other Side is fleeting. It is the same as the pain we go through arriving in this world, during birth. And just as babies very quickly forget the pain they endure emerging from the womb, so spirits erase the memories of their traumatic passing very soon after entering their new world.

I've had many encounters over the years that have underlined this belief. When I worked on the television series *Psychic Private Eyes*, for instance, I was in the presence of the spirits of several murder victims. One thing I did learn in my communications with these spirits was that the circumstances surrounding their passing were often a means for them to easily identify themselves. When I sense someone who has died of cancer, or of a sudden heart attack or stroke, for instance, I often feel breathlessness and a hot sensation in my skin. Similarly with murder victims I can feel anxiety and sometimes a sharp pain as we establish a connection.

But once that has happened, however, these spirits invariably tell me that their passing has been painless and that their new existence is a happy one.

The communications that I've had with these spirits also confirm that they go on to experience peaceful – and also productive – existences in spirit.

BROTHERLY LOVE

There are times when I am overawed by the power of love exerted by the spirit world. It really is the most intense and overwhelming force imaginable. I can think of few better examples of this than a young man called Eamonn. He was – and is – the embodiment of brotherly love. That love has helped him, and his family, overcome the truly tragic circumstances in which he passed over to spirit.

He first came to me in memorable circumstances. As I always tell my students and clients, spirits can wield a huge influence over a medium. Occasionally, for instance, I've been in the presence of a soul that is so powerful that I've started acquiring their characteristics and behaving like them without realising it. That's what happened with Eamonn one night when I was demonstrating in Ireland. It was quite a small venue, and I was demonstrating to a relatively small group of people – maybe two dozen. Without being aware of it, I began walking around the small stage area like a man. My shoulders were slouched and I had my hands in my pockets. It was very unladylike! It was only when I noticed the slightly shocked expression on some of the audience's faces that I sensed what was happening.

'Sorry about this,' I said. 'I seem to have been invaded by the spirit of a teenager.' I was actually wrong there; he was in his early twenties. As I tried to focus on his energy, the main image he was showing me was of a familiar Irish face – and voice – the old television presenter Eamonn Andrews who used to present *This Is Your Life* on television until the early 1990s. So I guessed that his name was Eamonn. I sensed that he'd passed quite recently. I also sensed he'd died an unpleasant death, almost as if he'd been poisoned.

It didn't take me long to connect with a lady who was sitting in the room. She identified the young man as her friend's son, Eamonn. When I asked her if she understood the circumstances surrounding his passing she nodded very slowly.

'Unfortunately I do, yes,' she said.

It was clear that he was here to connect with his mother through her friend and that he was being driven by an incredibly strong sense of purpose. I could feel that his mother had been in absolute despair at losing him and the lady before me knew that there several occasions when she hadn't wanted to go on. In fact, the only thing that had kept her going was her other son, John. Eamonn was determined to tell his mother, Marie, that she must carry on and that she had to look after John, and indeed the rest of the family.

As a mother myself, I could empathise totally with what Marie had gone through. I had a very strong feeling that Eamonn had more work to do. He really felt to me like a spirit who had been given a purpose on the Other Side.

And so it proved. Over the following months and years, Eamonn became a regular visitor when I was demonstrating and teaching. Most of the time this happened back here in England, with people who had no connection with him. So, along with my assistant Lucy, I struck up a friendship with Marie and her family. We agreed that if Eamonn passed on any messages that I believed were important to the family, we would call and pass them on.

One of Eamonn's other concerns was his brother, John. In the wake of his brother's death, John had become a real worry to his mother and the rest of the family. The family were worried that he could be influenced by those who had been an instrument to Eamonn's passing.

On one occasion, Eamonn came through at a workshop at my old centre, the Dragonfly Centre in

Waltham Abbey. He had been so concerned about John that he asked me to call his mother immediately. I'd asked Lucy to do it even before I'd finished the workshop that night. She'd spoken directly to John to tell him that he had to be careful. Eamonn had even warned about a particular guy, identifiable by a specific tattoo, that he needed to avoid at all costs. John was a sceptic, but had to take it seriously when a woman with whom he had no connection called him from the other side of the Irish Sea to pass on a warning from his brother.

He had gone very quiet when Lucy had passed on the message. But when she called him again a couple of times, he began to take her seriously. Since then he has slowly but surely cleaned up his act and is now a very proud father.

Eamonn still comes through to me in sittings even today. He regularly connects in order to gossip about his family and keep them on the straight and narrow. His is one of the most determined and driven souls I have ever encountered. He exemplifies how the soul can heal and become a power for good on the Other Side. Regardless of what its owner may have done with their life on this side.

PART SEVEN:
The Truth about Animals and the Afterlife

'If there are no dogs in Heaven, then
when I die I want to go where they went.'
Will Rogers

**Spirit Truth: our pets pass over to the
spirit world too**

Mediums tend to agree with each other on most subjects,
but there's one area that seems to divide them more than
any other. I've heard all sorts of arguments about what
happens to animals when they pass over.

Some, more traditional mediums, argue that, because
they aren't human, animals automatically go to a special

animal kingdom where they exist in a separate Afterlife of their own.

I personally disagree with this strongly. I believe there is an animal kingdom on the Other Side, but that this is reserved for animals who don't interact with us. So, for instance, this is where wild animals that live in the jungle or on the plains of Africa pass on to when they die. But it's my firm belief that the animals who share our lives with us here in this life pass over to the same Afterlife as us.

There are a couple of reasons why I believe this. The first is that this makes emotional and logical sense to me. Wild animals don't have a soul connection with us like our domestic pets do. Dogs, cats, horses, hamsters and budgies on the other hand are part of our lives. We love them, nurture them and give them our hearts. So for that reason, when they die they pass over to a place where they can be near to us and be close to our energy.

The second reason I believe this is more straight-forward: I have seen the evidence. Let me share with you a few of the most remarkable examples.

REGGIE, REGGIE

A couple of years ago I was very close to a personal trainer, Hayley. She was a huge help to me, not only getting me in shape for the demanding life I led travelling around the country, but also as a friend. She was a very sensitive and warm soul.

Hayley was a huge dog lover. She and her husband, Richard, had a pair of enormous Newfoundland dogs, or Newfies as she called them. The older of the dogs was called Leo and was Richard's dog from the period before he and Hayley got together.

The second dog, Reggie, was the dog they got together. They had bought him as a puppy from a breeder. He had grown up with them and was a real character. I remember once I was round at Hayley's house and she'd discovered him eating a bag of peanuts. How he'd got to them she had no idea. I couldn't help noticing that they were Reggae Reggae nuts so made a joke of it. 'Maybe he thought the packet said Reggie Reggie nuts,' I said. From then on I'd always called him Reggie Reggie.

Perhaps unsurprisingly, given that Hayley was a personal trainer, she and Richard were two very fit people and their dogs were active animals too. They would always go out as a family, running around the countryside and going on long walks together.

But then tragedy struck. When Reggie was still only a one-year-old, he was diagnosed with a serious liver condition. Hayley and Richard were really upset about it and spent a lot of time – and money – seeing vets. But the prognosis was always the same: Reggie wouldn't live much beyond his second birthday.

Hayley and Richard found it incredibly tough to deal with this. But they'd just about come to terms with it when they received more bad news. Leo had always been an active, healthy dog. But during a routine medical check-up their local vet found that he had a bad heart condition. He too was given a very short time to live.

The next few months were hellish for Hayley and Richard as they nursed not one but two dogs with what were, effectively, terminal illnesses. Leo was the first to die. Reggie died within seven or eight weeks of that.

It was an awful period for both of them, but Hayley was able to draw the strength to come through it from something that happened after the first of their dogs, Leo, passed away.

One night Hayley was woken up by movement in her bedroom. She looked across the bed to see a shadowy figure silhouetted in the gloom. It was sitting on the bed. At first she thought it was Richard sitting up and wondered if he was all right. But as her eyes adjusted to the darkness and she looked again, she saw it was something completely different. It was the spirit of Leo sitting on top of Richard.

Hayley is not a medium, but she's a sensitive woman and believes in the spirit world. She told me that it gave her huge strength. Reggie's final days were difficult ones as his liver condition worsened and he grew weaker. Having seen the spirit of Leo in the house, Hayley knew that Reggie's playmate was still there, keeping an eye not just on him but on Richard as well. Richard had taken the loss of Leo very badly. Hayley told Richard about seeing Leo but he didn't say much.

But there was no doubt in Hayley's mind that knowing Leo was present helped soften the blow when Reggie also passed over. Hayley knew that wherever Leo was, Reggie had now joined him. It gave her enormous comfort, I know.

SWEEP DREAMS

A similar thing happened to a friend of mine, Tracey. Like me she was a cat lover, and was particularly devoted to her cat, Sweep.

Sweep was an amazing cat. She'd had him for almost sixteen years, during which time he'd been through an enormous amount. At one point he'd been diagnosed with a tumour in his mouth. He'd needed an operation which cut away a section of his jaw and left him with a lop-sided mouth and a tongue that stuck out the side of his cheek.

Then Sweep had been involved in a freak shooting accident in which his pelvis and back leg had been shattered by an air gun. He'd had a metal plate and a pin inserted to keep him mobile. He'd walked really funnily but that hadn't bothered him – or Tracey, who adored him. In fact, everyone adored him, including the vets.

It was shortly before his sixteenth birthday that Sweep finally passed away. He had become weak and Tracey had taken the decision to have him put to sleep at the vets. But Sweep had decided to leave this life before that and died in Tracey's arms in the back of the car on the way to the surgery.

He had been in his favourite sleeping position, gazing at her. She was holding his paw when he passed. She told me how Sweep had given a gentle press on her hand then let out a little sigh before leaving. It was the most peaceful and beautiful passing.

Tracey missed his presence enormously that night, and for the next few days. But then something wonderful happened.

Tracey was lying in bed at night when she felt a familiar feeling. It was as if Sweep was walking across the bed, coming to rest next to her. She looked around but there was no sign of a cat – or anything else. At first she was very upset. She thought her mind was playing tricks with her.

But eventually she came to see that it was the spirit of her beloved cat.

Tracey had another cat, a quieter one called Honey.

She noticed a change in Honey's behaviour when Sweep left. One night soon after he'd passed over, Tracey was lying in bed crying. Honey came up to her and started licking the tears off her cheek. It was completely out of character.

It was then that she realised that the spirit of Sweep was at work in the house. That was something Sweep had done on a couple of occasions. How else would Honey have known to do this if Sweep's presence wasn't in the house telling her to? There was no way Honey would have done that otherwise.

The final confirmation came a few months later when,

for the second time, Tracey faced saying goodbye to one of her adored cats. Honey had now been diagnosed with a serious illness and the vets were recommending she be put to sleep.

Tracey was terribly upset. The night before she had to visit the vets to make a final decision, she was lying awake in bed, mulling over her options. She knew she had to do the right thing and put Honey out of her misery. But she was upset at the thought of being alone. How would she ever find another cat like Honey – let alone her beloved Sweep?

But then she felt those same, familiar footsteps on the bed. This time it was accompanied by a gentle thud, as if Sweep had plonked himself down on the duvet. At that point she realised she wasn't alone now, nor would she ever be. It made the following day – and days, weeks and months – so much easier to bear.

The ability of spirit animals to ease our pain is truly remarkable, I know from personal experience. Something similar happened to me with a pair of cats I had, sisters called Belle and Duff. Duff was a really affectionate character and the cuddliest cat you could wish to meet. She would snuggle up against me on the sofa, try to climb into my bed and generally follow me wherever I went. If I left home she'd miss me terribly.

Whenever I got back from a trip away she'd come out of the house to meet the car. As soon as I opened my car door she would jump in and leap on my shoulders.

I would have to walk into the house with her draped around my neck. By contrast, her sister Belle was very aloof. She was the embodiment of the independent, self-possessed cat. But when Duff passed, Belle's character changed completely. Suddenly she paid me attention in the way Duff had done. It was as if the spirit of Duff had somehow remained in the house and had been infused into Belle.

To me, what happened to Honey and Sweep – as well as Belle and Duff – offers indisputable evidence that the loving spirit of our pets remains with us always.

CINDERS

People are too dismissive of dreams. Far too often I've heard someone write off another person's description of something profound that has happened to them while they were asleep as 'just a dream'.

That's not true. The truth is that, for some people, dreams are the only way that a relative or a loved one can get through to them and be close to them from beyond the grave. There may be all sorts of obstacles stopping loved ones getting through when people are awake. It might be against their beliefs, for instance. They may also be too overwhelmed with emotions and grief. It may well be that it is easier for a spirit to connect and come forward when the person is in a dream state.

In fact, one of the subtlest ways in which spirits communicate with us is via dreams. The messages we receive in this way are often very simple ones. But that doesn't make them any less welcome, of course. These connections can be some of the most profound and powerful of all.

Last year I moved into a new house, a converted barn. I had all sorts of anxieties when I arrived there, some to do with the new home, but others to do with my professional and personal life. I was fast asleep and I dreamt of my nan flying high in the sky. I have a little marionette puppet of a witch flying. The reason I bought it is not because I am a witch myself, despite what some people may think, but because it looks like my nan. In my dream, she then flew all the way down to me, put her face close to mine and planted the softest of kisses on my cheek. It was such a real sensation that not only did I feel the kiss, I felt the creases on her face as she pressed her skin against me. I have absolutely no doubt in my mind that this was a simple message from her to say, 'I'm still here, and I still love you.' Nan was telling me that it would all be OK.

Spirit Truth: if you feel a physical connection in a dream it is a spirit connecting to you

---

I firmly believe that our pets are capable of connecting through our dreams as well. The example of a good friend of mine called Guy is, to my mind, proof of this.

As a young boy growing up, Guy was absolutely devoted to his Labrador-Retriever cross, Cinders or Cindy for short. Guy was a boy of only seven or eight years old when Cindy arrived in his home as a little black and grey bundle of barking energy. She was vivacious and extremely independent – and remained that way throughout her life, regularly running away.

Guy's parents did all they could to keep Cindy confined to the family home and garden, even erecting fences to keep her in. None of it worked. Guy told me once about how Cindy leapt twenty feet out of his bedroom window to escape. She always returned, of course, often arriving outside the house at 2 am, barking to be let back in. Guy always said that it was the Retriever in her.

He was a bit of a retriever himself. Sometimes Cindy would stay out for a little longer and Guy was always the person sent out to find and bring the dog home when she went missing like this. This forged an even deeper bond between him and Cindy, of course.

Guy was in his early twenties when he left home. Cindy was still part of the family, but was getting on a little by now. When he got a phone call from his mother telling him that his canine companion had passed away, he was devastated. He openly admitted to me that he was a wreck for days. It was no surprise. Cindy had been with the family nearly all his life – for seventeen years. It was no different to losing a human member of the household.

Guy is now in his forties. But he has never forgotten Cindy – and nor has Cindy forgotten him. Guy told me once that he regularly dreams about her.

The dreams vary but he and Cindy are always together, reunited, a little boy and his faithful friend. He sees her running around as she did when she was in her prime and can sometimes feel the brush of her coat on his skin.

He admitted that when he wakes up to realise that she is gone he is as devastated as he was twenty years earlier. He feels an immense, painful sense of loss.

My message to him was a simple one, however. I know that it is the spirit of Cindy communicating with him via his dreams. She misses him every bit as much as he misses her but is reaching out to him from the Other Side. Her messages are simple. He and Cindy aren't lost to each other at all.

THE PORK CHOP MYSTERY

Mediums often get messages from the spirit world via third parties, in particular from other psychics or mediums. I've received many of these over the years, often from the most unlikely sources. But few have been as unlikely – or as amusing – as the one that a student of mine delivered to me one evening as we took part in a workshop at my centre.

She was a promising student and was working with a circle of other developing mediums, taking it in turn to demonstrate their ability to connect with spirit. Practising like this in a circle is a really important part of any medium's apprenticeship and something that I'd done myself when I'd been developing years earlier. It's not easy, however – especially when you receive unorthodox communications, as she discovered that night.

She'd been a little confused when she'd first picked up on the energy of a spirit in the room, as can often be the case, even for experienced mediums like me. She knew she was in the presence of a male spirit, and was seeing the name John or Jack. But then she heard a snappy, barking sound.

'Could it be a dog?' she asked. I wasn't going to help her. I just signalled for her to carry on.

'I'm now being given the name Russ or Russell,' she continued. It took her a couple of moments to put two and two together. 'Oh, I think this is a Jack Russell dog,' she said. She described how she could see it munching away at something, looking nervously around as it did so.

The moment she said that, a memory from my past flashed up in my mind. However, I didn't say anything at this point as I wanted to see where it was going. When the student described how a little boy was crying because he was being blamed wrongly for something then I had to intervene.

'OK, this message is for me,' I said. 'This is my old Jack Russell. Go on. What else do you see?'

She then described how she had seen the dog grabbing something in its mouth from the top of a tall fridge or freezer, before jumping down onto the kitchen floor. She could smell a strong smell of meat, almost a barbecue aroma.

I couldn't help giggling.

'What's wrong?' she said. 'Did I get it wrong?'

'No, sorry,' I said. 'You've just solved a ten-year-old mystery.'

The incident that I was now replaying in my memory dated back more than a decade to the time when I was raising my sons James and Ryan on my own in Hoddesdon. One weekday evening I'd cooked three large pork chops for dinner. Money was tight at the time, so it was a bit of a treat.

I'm not the world's greatest cook. I can't cook more than one thing at a time. So having cooked the chops, I'd put them in a dish on top of the tall fridge freezer in the kitchen. I'd then set about getting the potatoes and vegetables ready.

The telephone in the hallway had rung at this point and I'd stepped out of the kitchen to answer it. I couldn't have been gone for more than a couple of minutes, but when I returned, I was furious to see that one of the chops was sitting in the middle of the kitchen floor. Not only that, but someone had taken several large bites out of it.

I went ballistic and immediately blamed my oldest son, James, who was sitting in the living room next door watching television. He protested his innocence and blamed our dog, a little Jack Russell called Pippa, which we'd acquired from a friend. I was completely in love with this dog. It was such a cute, cuddly character, butter wouldn't melt in its mouth as far as I was concerned.

'Don't try and push the blame onto the poor little dog,' I'd said. 'She's way too small to get up onto the top of the fridge and then get a pork chop onto the floor.'

I'd felt guilty about it afterwards, because I'd given James such an ear-bashing he'd burst into tears. He'd sat at the dinner table that night with red eyes – and minus his pork chop, which had gone in the bin.

'What else did you see?' I asked my student at the end of the exercise.

'I saw the dog jumping on a chair and then climbing up on top of something,' she said.

The penny dropped in my head. I must have used a chair to get something out of a cupboard and then left it in a position where the dog could use it as a stepping stone onto the worktop and from there to the fridge freezer. It had obviously climbed up using the chair and then picked the chop up with its teeth and lobbed it onto the floor where it had taken a few chunks before I reappeared.

I rang James later that night and issued him an apology, ten years too late. I'm sure that at first he thought I'd gone completely and utterly mad. But then he remembered the incident. I don't know which one of us laughed the loudest.

BELLA

The friendships we form with our pets can be some of the strongest we make in our entire lives. So it's no surprise that many of us want to continue those friendships in the spirit world.

A perfect illustration of this is my paternal grandmother, my nan. As I've mentioned, I was very close to her from the time I was a little girl until a few years ago, when she passed over at the grand old age of ninety-one.

I had a difficult childhood growing up in Enfield, north London. I had a volatile relationship with my mother and my parents separated when I was very young. As a result of this, I spent a lot of time round at my nan's house, a short distance away from our home. I'd often head there after school, spending a few hours at her kitchen table. She was my rock, the person to whom I clung the most. She was also the person who first sensed my ability or 'second sight', as she called it.

As I say, my nan lived to ninety-one, far outlasting my granddad, with whom she didn't really get on, to be fair. It was a two-way street – he didn't get on with her either. I always joke that my granddad reincarnated as a tortoise to get away from her!

During the final few years of her life, my nan's closest companion was her dog, Bella. She had always been fond of dogs and had a lot of them over the years. But Bella was special. She was a black and white Border Collie and my nan was absolutely devoted to her. She spoke to Bella all the time, as if she was a person. They were as inseparable as a married couple who had been together for fifty years. So it wasn't a surprise that the two of them left us within a few weeks of each other.

Bella was the first to pass. She was quite elderly and had to be put to sleep. Making the decision to euthanise her beloved pet was really hard for my nan. She was a tough lady on the outside, but inside she had a heart of absolute gold and that heart broke when she had to sign the permission slip for the vet to administer the injection. She'd been there with Bella as she'd slipped away.

There's no doubt in my mind that it helped hasten her own departure from this life. Bella was put to sleep in the February. My nan passed over the following month, in March, on Mother's Day to be precise. I was fairly certain that the two of them were going to be together on the Other Side and it didn't take long to have that confirmed.

One evening I was working with some of my students when one of them said she could feel the presence of a grandmother. She said she could also sense that she was close to me. 'I feel like I've got your nan here,' she said.

My job as a teacher is to encourage my students to interpret what they are sensing accurately and in detail, but to do so under their own steam. So I wasn't going to help her. I just sat there impassively. I'd need a lot more evidence to persuade me this was my nan, I said to myself.

But then the student just blurted out the name Bella.

'She's with a dog, she's called Bella,' she said. 'Do you understand what that means?'

'Yes, I understand that you really have got my nan with you,' I said, to her delight, not just that she'd done so well, but that she'd made contact with such an important person in my life.

She went on to pass on a lovely message from my nan about how she and Bella had found each other soon after she'd passed over to the Other Side. There were mentions of other members of her family too, some of whom I'd never known. But it was clear that Bella was her constant companion.

It made perfect sense to me. As I say, my nan and my granddad were far from the perfect couple. They essentially lived separate lives towards the end of my granddad's time here. Bella was a far more significant figure, certainly in my nan's twilight years. So it was no surprise to discover that they had been reunited on the Other Side.

I've had a few students claim that they're in the presence of my nan since then. Unless they have Bella with her, I don't believe them.

IN THE CLOUDS

I'm shown all sorts of weird and wonderful images by the spirit world, but one of the most curious appeared in my mind when I was demonstrating on stage in Hayes a year or two ago.

Early on during the evening I was aware that an elderly lady was trying to connect with me. She was showing me an image of herself in a park, walking with what I could only describe as a cloud attached to a lead. I really couldn't make head nor tail of what it was for a few moments, but then I heard a barking noise. It was a dog, I realised. It had a huge, puffy, white coat and was padding along with this lady beside a lake in the park.

I'm more of a cat person than a dog one and am not very good at recognising different breeds, so I put it out to the audience. 'Would anyone understand a lady walking a dog that looks just like a cloud?' I asked, drawing ripples of laughter.

Almost instantly, however, a hand went up. It was a youngish woman, sitting towards the side of the theatre. 'Yes, I think that might be my mum,' she said.

'OK. So what sort of dog would this be then?'

'It's a Bichon Frisé,' she said. 'My mum had a lovely Bichon Frisé that she was absolutely devoted to.'

I felt pretty certain that I had made the right connection so began to pass on the information that this lady was giving me. I sensed that she'd died suddenly of a heart-related illness. I also sensed that her dog might have been with her when she passed. The young woman nodded and smiled at all this. The main message had already been given, in a way. This dog was clearly very dear to the lady and they had now been reunited on the Other Side.

After the demonstration I spoke briefly to the young woman who confirmed that I'd been pretty accurate in the picture I'd drawn. Her mother had lived alone for the final years of her life and had endured quite a lot of emotional heartache. The daughter lived a long way away from her mum so couldn't be there as often as she'd have liked. She had a career and a family of her own to care for as well. So the dog had been her mother's lifeline. He was her constant companion, the one who gave her the unconditional love that she needed.

Her mum had died of a massive heart attack while out walking the dog in their favourite park. By the time paramedics had reached her it was too late.

The dog had been absolutely shattered by her passing. The daughter had been unable to look after it so it had been sent to an animal sanctuary and then on to another home. But it hadn't been happy there and became unwell. It died within months of its devoted owner.

It's common for people to come through to let loved ones know that they have been reunited with someone important on the Other Side, whether it's their child or parent or husband or wife. This lady wanted me to reassure her daughter that she was with the most important individual in her life. It was a hugely comforting message for her daughter.

CHUBBY CHEEKS

People often ask me what is the strangest thing I have witnessed while I have been communicating with the spirit world. It's a difficult question to answer in some ways. It depends on your understanding of the word strange. I've seen some pretty odd things! For sheer bizarreness, however, few sights will ever compete with the one I saw one evening when I was demonstrating at a church in Brighton.

It was a very small, intimate venue, down a tiny alleyway. It could only hold fifty people so it was packed out, mostly with regular members of the church. As I've explained before, I'm not a member of the Spiritualist – or any other – church, so I could tell some of the audience were a little bit wary of me at first, especially when I began conducting the demonstration in my normal, light-hearted way. To be honest, I don't think most of them had seen anything like me before. Despite this, however, there was a really good atmosphere in the room, mainly because it was such a small and intense environment. Once they'd got used to me, the audience began having fun. I was soon living up to my occasional billing as a 'comedium'.

For some reason, my mind was full of images of animals that evening and I had quite a lot of communications from cats that had passed over. I could tell that this was a bit much for some of the more traditional members of the church. So goodness knows what these people made of the message I got towards the end of the evening.

I felt myself being drawn to a middle-aged lady who was sitting towards the front of the church. As I spoke to her I was aware of something scurrying around on the stage next to me. I looked down and realised it was a hamster.

'I've got a hamster here with me, do you understand that?' I said to this lady, giggling.

'Yes, I do,' she said.

I had several other spirits trying to make their way through to me so I didn't dwell on this. Besides, the hamster was making me giggle too much, which isn't always conducive to good mediumship. The hamster had other ideas, however.

As I was about to move on to another message that was taking shape in my head, I sensed a figure standing somewhere in the church. I couldn't believe my eyes when I looked up. On the right-hand side of the church there was another hamster – a giant hamster. The shock must have been written all over my face. It was like a scene out of the classic television series *The Goodies* where they'd often have a giant kitten that was taller than the GPO tower in London. This hamster must have been at least six feet tall. All I could see was its chubby cheeks and a large, white dot on its nose. It was as if it was trying to force me to look at it.

I got the really strong sense that it was hungry. It was all I could do to stop myself laughing out loud. But I knew I couldn't because it was clearly here to pass on a serious message. I returned to the lady and asked her if the fact that the hamster seemed very hungry meant anything to her. She nodded.

I was then shown images of a little boy in tears. This

again drew a nod from the lady. It turned out that the hamster was in spirit and needed to get a message to the boy, this lady's grandson. The hamster had been his favourite pet and had passed a week earlier. He'd been devastated by this and blamed himself for it. His parents had wondered whether he hadn't been feeding it properly.

The spirit of the hamster was confirming that their suspicions had been correct. But it was also passing on a more optimistic message. Yes, he had died because they hadn't been looking after him correctly. But it was determined to tell me that it was safe and well in spirit and the family didn't need to beat themselves up about neglecting it. The lady smiled warmly at this and said she'd pass the message on to her grandson.

And with that the giant hamster faded from my view, clearly content that its message had been successfully passed on. It was a message I won't forget in a hurry, I have to admit. How could I?

Spirit Truth: **spirits understand the reality – sometimes better than we do**

A common mistake that many people make is to assume that, because our loved ones have crossed over to the spirit world, they no longer understand or appreciate the reality of life here in this world. That couldn't be further from the truth. Spirits, if anything, have a clearer grasp of reality than we do. They see things as they really are – and aren't afraid to tell us. A couple of stories exemplify this.

TOP DOG

It's not unusual for me to sense the presence of more than one spirit standing alongside me on the stage when I am demonstrating. It often happens. The pair of spirits that materialised one evening when I was working with a congregation of about 120 people in a church in Basingstoke, however, was unusual.

At first I felt the presence of a man. He'd been passed a few months and was in his early sixties. I quickly sensed his name – Brian. He immediately felt like a husband or a father, that's the way his energy was presenting itself to me. So far, so perfectly normal. Well for me, at least!

But I was soon being made aware of another presence standing in front of Brian. It was smaller physically but wasn't a child. I looked down and saw that it was a dog. As I say, I'm not great with breeds, but I recognised this one because it was a little Yorkshire Terrier. A friend of mine has one named Susie, one of the loveliest dogs I've ever met.

Ordinarily when you get the spirit of a human and an animal together it suggests there was a special bond between them in this life. That wasn't the case here, however. From the moment they appeared, I sensed that Brian and the Yorkie were together slightly reluctantly. I wasn't in the presence of a man and his best friend. As the message began to take shape, I began to understand why.

Brian was quite a comical character; he had a very dry sense of humour. I was getting a very strong sense that a woman, possibly his wife, and possibly called Sandra, was in the audience, waiting to connect with him. But he was making it clear that he didn't want to connect with her until I had dealt with the dog. 'Get the mutt sorted first,' he said, tongue-in-cheek, to me.

I explained the situation to the audience and suggested that the dog and the man were looking for a lady called Sandra. I was drawn to a lady in the second row so I asked her, 'Do you understand this message about the dog?'

'Yes, I do,' she said.

I sensed that this little dog had been put to sleep recently because of old age. She nodded at this. Despite the fact that it wasn't close to Brian, there was a lovely glow about the dog. I got the feeling that it was very happy. This made her quite emotional. She kept saying 'thank you' and dabbing away at her eyes.

The dog showed me a few images of her walking him in a local wood. I then saw them returning home, the dog splattered in mud and soaking wet, but with Sandra smiling broadly. She had really loved spending time with the dog – that was abundantly obvious.

As this image faded, however, so did the energy of the dog. I got the feeling that it had conveyed its very simple message. Brian clearly knew this as well and was now ready to take centre stage, as it were. Sandra confirmed that Brian was her husband. He'd passed some time before the dog, but there wasn't a huge time gap between them, I sensed. 'That's right,' she said. 'Brian passed three months earlier.'

I joked that she didn't seem as emotional about being reunited with Brian as she had been about hearing from the spirit of her dog. She laughed at this, as did Brian.

'It was exactly the same in life, you thought more of the dog than you did of me,' he said. 'I saw how much you spent on the funeral.'

She laughed at this. I could tell it was how he had spoken to her in life. He'd not changed now that he was in the spirit world.

'But that's fine. I always understood that,' he said. 'I didn't want you to spend money on my funeral either. It was lovely, and you did me proud. But I'd have been happy if you'd gone to B&Q and just made up a box out of MDF and stuck that in the hole. In fact, I'd have been happy if you'd put me in a bin bag.'

Again, she chuckled at this.

The message he wanted to get across was twofold, really. Deep down, I sensed, there was great love between them. You could feel it in the humour, the banter between them. She must have missed that enormously, but here it was 'live' in a theatre.

But he also wanted to show his love by letting her know that her beloved dog was safe as well. Brian made it clear that he was with the dog reluctantly. It was as if he was looking after it until Sandra joined him. It was an act of selfless love on his behalf, but it was also an act of realism. He knew that she felt very differently about him than she did about her Yorkie. But if looking after the dog was his best way of ensuring he was reunited with her, he was happy to do it. It was an example of how honest the spirit world is. It doesn't present a rose-coloured view of things. It tells it as it is. And that's what Brian had come to do.

Spirit Truth: **a message from an animal can transform people's lives**

The importance of pets to people cannot be over-estimated. I've come across many people who have been more devastated by the loss of a favourite cat, dog or other pet than they have been over the loss of a husband, brother or parent. Well, on the surface at least.

There is, I believe, a reason why people react so strongly to the loss. Yes, of course, the idea that they have lost a friend is shattering. And there's no question that some people do have a greater affinity for their animals than they do for humans. I think that's tied in to the fact that animals can't answer back and offer the kind of unquestioning, unconditional love that you rarely, if ever, get between humans.

But I think the loss runs deeper than that. I think on a psychological level, animals act as a great outlet for our emotions. When we feel angry, sad, frustrated or lonely, we can lift the weight simply by walking and playing with the dog or lying on the sofa curled up with the cat. So it is completely understandable that when that outlet is taken away it can throw us completely out of control emotionally.

A man I encountered down in Wales a couple of years ago embodied this very well indeed.

I met him at a rather special place, Hafan-y-Coed, near Swansea. A simple, unpretentious but rather beautiful spiritual centre in the Welsh hillsides, it had become an important place for me spiritually. A year or two before this encounter, I'd had something of an epiphany there. I'd made the long drive down the M4, planning to quit teaching because it was such a drain on my other work. When you are responsible for other mediums and their development, you can sometimes forget about your own development. I felt I was losing ground and – basically – losing my grip on my mediumship by teaching so much. I'd arrived at Hafan-y-Coed determined that it would be the last time I taught. Fittingly there was a sign on the wall as I arrived welcoming me to 'the land of new beginnings'. It was certainly that. By the end of my week teaching ten wonderful people I'd changed my mind completely. I was revived and ready to teach all over again.

So I'd gone back down there on this occasion with a real spring in my step. I think it showed in some of the sittings that I did that week. Early on I met this lovely man. I sensed immediately that he was in the presence of the spirit of an elderly lady. It was his mother, who had passed quite recently. When I explained this he nodded and smiled gently. He was clearly pleased to hear from her, but there was something in his reaction that told me he was disappointed. He was waiting for something else.

As the sitting progressed, I began to hear some music. Perhaps it was the Welsh connection, but it was the unmistakable voice of Tom Jones. He was singing 'What's New Pussycat?' I then felt a different energy emerging. It was a beautiful, ginger cat.

The man was a very peaceful, gentle soul. He was a gardener and actually worked keeping the beautiful grounds at Hafan-y-Coed looking as good as they did. When I told him that I had a ginger cat with me it was like the sun had coming up in the morning. His face just lit up in a beautiful glow.

I told him that the cat was with his mother and that they were both at peace in spirit. This made him incredibly happy. He left the room a different man. The connection had taken a huge weight off his shoulders.

We spoke again over the course of the week that I spent there. I'd see him almost every day when I walked the grounds after breakfast. One day we had a little chat and he told me a bit more about his circumstances. He was a bachelor and had lived with his mother until her death. He had been all at sea when she passed. His little tomcat, Eddie, had been the centre of his universe, his only point of contact with another living creature.

'I told that cat more about the way I felt than the local vicar or any of my relatives or friends,' he admitted to me. 'It was silly really, but it was unconditional friendship and unconditional love.'

So when the cat had become ill with a tumour in its brain, he had been absolutely devastated. He'd had to make the decision to put Eddie down himself and had found it very tough. Taking the cat to the vet to be given an injection was one of the hardest things he'd ever had to do in his life, he told me.

'Of course, losing my mother was a bigger moment in my life. But somehow losing Eddie felt worse. I almost feel guilty saying that,' he said.

As we chatted I suggested to him that he had been grieving for his mum through his cat. So when Eddie had passed he had suddenly felt all alone. He had nowhere to put his grief any more, there was none of the unconditional love he'd needed when he'd lost his mother.

It confirmed for me once more how powerful that bond between humans and animals can be. Many people don't understand it, but he did – and, after talking to him, I had a better understanding of it too.

EPILOGUE:
Extra Time

No matter how much of your life you spend in the company of spirit, there are times when you realise that it is more powerful and mysterious than you will ever understand. The truth is that it can act in ways that are beyond the comprehension of any of us.

I suppose, in many cases, these events are what some people would call miracles. They are so outside what we call normality that they can only be seen in that way.

The experience I and my colleagues went through in the company of one of my regular students not that long ago certainly fell into this category. It was a miracle.

A group of sixteen students of different ages and abilities were taking part in a week-long course at my centre. One of the group was a regular at my centre. I will call her Amanda. From the Monday, Amanda was being connected to spirits who were repeatedly passing on the same message about her grandson. His name was Ross and he was terminally ill because of a lung condition caused by a serious medical accident when he was a baby. He was just five years old and, after many years in and out of hospital, was now confined to a hospice. His condition had deteriorated to such an extent that he had a DNR – Do Not Resuscitate – notice on his bed. Amanda, like everyone else in the family, had begun to prepare herself for the worst and accept that Ross was entering his final days.

The messages coming through suggested that the end was drawing very close. Amanda spoke to her family and told us that Ross had developed pneumonia and his lungs were filling up with water. There was very little they could do for him. It was a matter of time.

I was away for the first part of the course, which was run by my assistant Lucy. I joined them on the Friday. It was an extraordinary day, one I won't forget in a hurry. I didn't know anything about the messages that had been pouring in about Ross. So when I connected with a spirit early during the day, I had to let the others fill me in. Throughout the morning, virtually every message we got related to this little boy in one way or another. But then something truly extraordinary happened.

Halfway through the afternoon, after we'd had a brief coffee break, we were all back in the room where we'd been working together. Everyone told me that the energy there had been quite intense for the past five days. It had certainly felt that way during the morning. There was a lot of energy there again when we resumed, but about ten minutes later it disappeared. And when I say it disappeared, I mean every molecule of it just vanished. I had never felt anything like it.

One moment we could all feel spirit all around us, the next it had gone. It was as if the whole room had shut down, as if someone somewhere had hit a giant 'off' switch or told the assembled spirits to abandon the house because it was on fire. Every single spirit person that was in the room had left as one. We persevered for a few minutes but it was soon obvious that it was a waste of everyone's time. I decided to call it a day and told all sixteen students to go home for the weekend.

'I've got a feeling they've all been dispatched to this little boy that they are all so worried about,' I told Lucy and a couple of others as we cleared up the room.

'Maybe he's about to pass over and they are going to meet him,' someone suggested.

'I'm not so sure,' I said. 'That doesn't quite make sense to me. I have a feeling there's something else going on.'

I kept thinking about it throughout the weekend. It was quietly nagging away at the back of my mind. When I got to the studio on Monday morning, the first thing I did was to email Amanda. I got a reply almost instantly. She told me that the weekend had been the most incredible of her life – and that of her family.

On Friday night, Ross's parents had arrived at the hospice expecting to find their son in the same condition they'd left him in that morning. To their surprise, however, he'd been sitting up and breathing much better than he had been.

The doctors were puzzled by what had happened. They said they were going to run some tests over the weekend, but his pneumonia seemed to have stabilised. By Monday, the news was even better. Ross had slept well on Friday night and improved further through Saturday. By Sunday he was showing no signs of pneumonia or anything else that posed an immediate threat to his life.

His lung condition remained something that he would not recover from long-term. But for now the prognosis was much better. The doctors had even recommended that Ross be discharged from the hospice.

Needless to say, the family was in a state of shock, as were we. But as that day wore on I began to realise what had happened on Friday afternoon.

There was no doubt in my mind that the spirit world had been agitated. As they said in the *Star Wars* movies, 'there is a great disturbance in the Force'. As we had witnessed ourselves, on Friday afternoon they had all downed tools and forgotten what they were doing and headed somewhere else.

Now the big question was: why?

I was fascinated to know precisely what was motivating spirit. Why had they done this? Why hadn't they allowed this little boy to pass at this point, especially if it was just a matter of time before he joined them?

When I got to talk to Amanda again, I learned a lot more about her relatives' predicament. It provided a few more pieces in the jigsaw. The truth was that caring for their son had left them in a really precarious situation.

They lived in a council house and were struggling financially, partly because they had to spend so much time travelling back and forth to hospitals and now the hospice. They were behind with their rent and were now being threatened with eviction.

Ironically, the only thread of hope for them lay with their son. Their lawyers had told them that they were almost certainly eligible for a major compensation award because the hospital was responsible for his illness. They would be awarded the money that they would need to care for Ross properly, twenty-four hours a day. The sum would run into hundreds of thousands of pounds.

They were due to go to court any day, but if Ross died, the case would be abandoned. The family would not have had any compensation and would almost certainly have become homeless.

There was no doubt in my mind that this is why the spirit world was so agitated. They were trying to save this poor family from an awful fate. They must have known that Ross had to be alive for them to be eligible for money for his ongoing care. The compensation would also allow them to buy a new home.

The longer Ross survived, the more chance the family would have of making a life when he did leave them – and of course the more time they would have to be with him.

Ross won't ever recover because that's not possible. But he may now have been given an extra couple of years. And that may be what the spirits want for this little boy and his parents.

*

The spirit world never ceases to surprise, amaze and inspire me. During the course of my career as a medium I've regularly seen, heard and felt things that have been beyond my expectations – and beyond my understanding too. One of the greatest lessons I've learned is to accept that this is fine. Sometimes I never will understand. I simply need to keep doing what I do. The spirit world will look after the rest.

This is the final thought I would like to share with you. The spirits of our loved ones are among us and around us, always. As, hopefully, I've explained, we don't need to be mediums or psychics to experience the spirit world.

The truth is that none of us will ever comprehend the spirit world fully. But we don't need to. We simply need to be open-minded, honest and courageous enough to be ready for the messages and connections it brings us. If we do that, we can all experience true spirit . . .